"ATTACKS ON LINKING" REVISITED

International Psychoanalytical Association's Psychoanalytic Classics Revisited Series

Series Editor: Gennaro Saragnano

Other titles in the Series

Playing and Reality Revisited
edited by Gennaro Saragnano and Christian Seulin

"ATTACKS ON LINKING" REVISITED

A New Look at Bion's Classic Work

edited by

Catalina Bronstein and
Edna O'Shaughnessy

Routledge
Taylor & Francis Group
LONDON AND NEW YORK

First published 2017 by Karnac Books Ltd.

Published 2018 by Routledge
2 Park Square, Milton Park, Abingdon, Oxon OX14 4RN
711 Third Avenue, New York, NY 10017, USA

Routledge is an imprint of the Taylor & Francis Group, an informa business

British Library Cataloguing in Publication Data

A C.I.P. for this book is available from the British Library

ISBN 9781782203032 (pbk)

Edited, designed and produced by The Studio Publishing Services Ltd
www.publishingservicesuk.co.uk
email: studio@publishingservicesuk.co.uk

CONTENTS

ACKNOWLEDGEMENTS

We would like to express our gratitude to all those people who have contributed to the publication of this book.

We are grateful to our colleagues of the Publications Committee of the International Psychoanalytical Association and in particular to its Chair, Gennaro Saragnano, for his support and encouragement. Special mention should also go to Rhoda Bawdekar from the IPA. Our gratitude also goes to Liz Allison and Phillip Birch who helped with the editing of some of the chapters.

We are grateful to The Marsh Agency Ltd on behalf of the estate of W. R. Bion for permission to print pages 93–109 of Chapter 8 (Attacks on linking) and pages 162–166 of Chapter 10 (Commentary) from *Second Thoughts: Selected papers on Psycho-Analysis* by Wilfred Bion (originally published by Jason Aronson Inc. in 1967).

Our gratitude also goes to Kate Pearce and the team at The Studio for their help with manuscripts, proofs and getting the book ready.

Finally, but not least, our gratitude goes to all the contributors who have generously made this publication possible.

Catalina Bronstein and Edna O'Shaughnessy

IPA PUBLICATIONS COMMITTEE

The Publications Committee of the International Psychoanalytical Association continues, with this volume, the series "Psychoanalytic Classics Revisited".

The aim of this new series of books, which follows the four successful series previously published under the auspices of the International Psychoanalytical Association, is to make available to psychoanalysts, and other scholars in related fields, a reinterpretation of the classics of psychoanalysis by authoritative colleagues from various countries and with different theoretical approaches in the light of the more recent developments in contemporary psychoanalysis.

In a historical period characterised by the increased internationalisation of psychoanalysis, and its rapid spread in Eastern Europe and Asia, we believe that there is an increased demand for psychoanalytical culture and for further investigating the great classics of this discipline, whether books or single papers, which have marked the history of the theoretical and clinical development of psychoanalysis. We think that the word "Classics" includes all those contributions which, far from being comprehensible only if viewed against a specific historical and cultural backdrop, are capable of continuously revealing to us their capacity of stimulating psychoanalytical thought in a creative and anti-dogmatic manner, and, therefore, remain as inalienable theoretical and clinical landmarks, regardless of the personal opinions and approach of each psychoanalyst.

As clear and enriching as it is, "Attacks on Linking" *Revisited. A New Look at Bion's Classic Work,* edited by Catalina Bronstein and Edna O'Shaughnessy, greatly fulfils the aim of this book series. Wilfred R. Bion's impressive description of the functioning of the psychotic parts of human personality certainly represents one of the most important "classics" of our discipline, which, as Jay Greenberg states in his Foreword to the book, has influenced psychoanalysts and students from all over the world, regardless of their different theoretical approaches. In this volume, a selected group of very distinguished colleagues revisits Bion's text in the light of our contemporary psychoanalytic thinking, thus providing us with an excellent "new look" at this classic work.

Gennaro Saragnano, MD
Series Editor
Chair, IPA Publications Committee

ABOUT THE EDITORS AND CONTRIBUTORS

Editors

Catalina Bronstein is President of the British Psychoanalytical Society and Visiting Professor in the Psychoanalysis Unit, University College, London. She is a training and supervising analyst of the British Psychoanalytical Society She is a child, adolescent and adult psychoanalyst. She is the former London Editor of the *International Journal of Psychoanalysis* and is currently a member of the Board of the IJP. She is also a member of the Publications Committee of the International Psychoanalytical Association. She has written numerous papers and chapters in books and monographs and has edited *Kleinian Theory, A Contemporary Perspective* and co-edited *The New Klein–Lacan Dialogues*. She works in London in private practice and at the Brent Adolescent Centre.

Edna O'Shaughnessy was born in South Africa in 1924. After the Second World War, she came to England to continue her studies in philosophy at the University of Oxford. Questions that specially engaged her, and on which she wrote, were meaning and its representation, and the freedom—or not—to choose, both topics of continuing interest when she moved from philosophy to psychoanalysis in the 1950s. Her analytic training began with children at the Tavistock Clinic. Then, in the 1960s, she trained as a psychoanalyst for adults at the British Psychoanalytical Society, of which she is now a Distinguished Fellow, a training and supervising analyst, and a child analyst. For a while now, she has not seen patients (a huge loss) but she still does some supervisory work with analysts and psychotherapsts and in the Tavistock's Fitzjohn's Unit, where psychodynamic treatment is offered to adults suffering chronic mental health problems. During more than fifty years of psychoanalytic work, Edna O'Shaughnessy has written many papers, now published as her collected papers.

Contributors

Christine Anzieu-Premmereur has a PhD in Psychology, is an adult and child psychiatrist, an adult and child psychoanalyst, and a member of the Société Psychanalytique de Paris. She moved from Paris to New York on 2000. She is a member of the faculty at the Columbia Psychoanalytic Center for Training and Research, where she is the director of the Parent–Infant Psychotherapy Training Program, and Assistant Clinical Professor in Psychiatry at the Columbia University. She is a member of the New York Psychoanalytic Institute, and chairs the discussion group on Parent–Infant Programs at Psychoanalytic Institutes at the American Psychoanalytic Association meetings. She has a private practice in New York as an adult and child psychoanalyst. She also consults with parents and babies. She has published two books in French, on play in child psychotherapy and on psychoanalytic interventions with parents and babies, many papers in English on child psychoanalysis, motherhood, and symbolisation process, and, recently, chapters on the process of representation in early childhood, and on the capacity to dream and night terrors in children.

Rachel B. Blass is a member and training analyst of the Israel Psychoanalytic Society and a member of the British Psychoanalytical Society. She is a Professor at Heythrop College, University of London and editor of the "Controversies" section of the *International Journal of*

Psychoanalysis. She has published a book and over 70 articles which deal mainly with the conceptual, epistemological, and ethical foundations of psychoanalysis and their relevance to contemporary analytic thinking and practice. Many of her writings study the development of Freud's ideas and how Kleinian analysis grounds and advances them. She has lectured, taught, and offered workshops and clinical seminars in many countries and her papers have been translated into 15 languages.

Ronald Britton is a Fellow of the Royal College of Psychiatrists and Distinguished Fellow of the British Psychoanalytical Society, he was given the International Psychoanalytical Association Award for Outstanding Scientific Contributions in July 2013 and the Sigourney Award for Distinguished Contributions to Psychoanalysis in January 2014. His books include, *The Oedipus Complex Today; Belief and Imagination; Sex, Death and the Superego; Between Mind and Brain*. Although essentially a clinical practitioner, his writing has emphasised the relationship of analysis to literature, philosophy, and theology

Elias Mallet da Rocha Barros: is a training analyst and supervisor of the Brazilian Association of Psychoanalysis of São Paulo (SBPSP), member of its faculty; Fellow of the British Psychoanalytical Association and of its Institute; Past Editor for the Latin America of the *International Journal Of Psychoanalysis*, Past Chair of CAPSA-IPA, Chair for Latin America of the Task Force for the Encyclopedia and Dictionary organised by the IPA, and member of the Editorial Board of seven journals. He has received the Sigourney Award for distinguished contributions to psychoanalysis in 1999.

Elizabeth Lima da Rocha Barros is a training analyst and supervisor of the Brazilian Association of Psychoanalysis of São Paulo (SBPSP), member of its faculty, Fellow of the British Psychoanalytical Association and of its Institute, child psychotherapist at the Tavistock Clinic, child analyst at the British Psychoanalytical Association, Past Co-Editor of the *Journal of Psychoanalysis* (SBPSP), and has a DEA in Psychopathology from The Sorbonne, Université René Descartes.

Antonino Ferro is President of the Italian Psychoanalytic Society and also Consultant Associate Editor of the *International Journal of Psychoanalysis*. He is a training and supervising analyst in the Italian Psychoanalytic Society, the American Psychoanalytic Association and the International Psychoanalytic Association. He has been a visiting professor of psychoanalysis in various institutions in Europe, North America, South America, and Australia. He received the Sigourney Award in 2007.

Jay Greenberg: training and supervising analyst at the William Alanson White Institute. He is the Editor of *The Psychoanalytic Quarterly* and former Editor for North America of the *International Journal of Psychoanalysis*. Also, former Editor of *Contemporary Psychoanalysis*. He is the co-author with Stephen Mitchell of *Object Relations in Psychoanalytic Theory*. He is also the author of *Oedipus and Beyond: A Clinical Theory*. He was the recipient in 2015 of the Mary S. Sigourney Award for outstanding achievement in psychoanalysis.

Monica Horovitz, MD, PhD of Letters, MA in Latin American Literature, DESS in clinical psychopathology, born in Buenos Aires, is a full member of the Paris Psychoanalytic Society (SPP) and of the Italian Psychoanalytical Society (SPI). She works in private practice with adolescents and adults in Paris. For the past twelve years, she has run a seminar on Bion. She is the Chair of the international seminar on Bion called "Bion in Marrakesh" that was initiated with Lawrence Brown in 2013. She has published a number of articles in national and international journals, such as: *Revue Française de Psychanalyse, Psychanalyse et Psychose, Publications SPADEA; International Journal of Psychoanalysis, Caliban, revista de la FEPAL,* among others. She has also contributed to several books published in French, English, and Spanish, on the works of Wilfred Bion,

Clara Nemas, MD, IPA, is a training and supervising analyst of the Buenos Aires Psychoanalytic Association (APdeBA), child and adolescent psychoanalyst, and a member of the International Psychoanalytical Association. She maintains a full-time private psychoanalytic practice in Buenos Aires, and was vice-president and scientific secretary of the APdeBA. She chairs the admissions and progression committee of the IPA China Committee, and serves on the editorial board of the *International Journal of Psychoanalysis*. She is also a member of the Latin American Working Party on Comparative Clinical Methods. She has published numerous papers on ethics, psychoanalytic theory, and clinical technique in working with adolescent patients, and is currently involved in teaching Kleinian and neo-Kleinian theory.

Rudi Vermote, MD, PhD, is a psychoanalyst, training analyst, past president of the Belgian Society of Psychoanalysis, and a member of the editorial board of the *International Journal of Psychoanalysis*. He is the head of the Psychoanalytic Psychotherapy Unit for Personality Disorders (KLIPP) at the Psychiatric Centre of the University of Leuven, Campus Kortenberg, and Associate Professor at the Faculty of Medicine and the Faculty of Psychology at the University of Leuven. Head of the postgraduate training in psychoanalytic psychotherapy at the University of Leuven, his research projects involve the link between process and clinical outcome in psychotherapy and clinical research on the different facets of mentalization in personality disorders. He has published and presented papers on Bion's work at several congresses and is the author of *Reading Bion* in the teaching series of Routledge (series editor Dana Birksted-Breen), which is in publication.

FOREWORD

Jay Greenberg

In the history of psychoanalysis there are only a handful of papers that have shifted the centre of gravity of thinking not only within their own theoretical communities but within other traditions as well. Bion's "Attacks on linking" is surely one such paper; there is virtually no place in the contemporary analytic world that has not been touched by the many ideas that are presented, often schematically and even somewhat obscurely, within its few pages. Its ideas have influenced and been elaborated upon not only by the London Kleinians who were Bion's colleagues and students, but by authors coming from other conceptual starting points—North American relationalists, Latin American and European field theorists, even some restless ego psychologists.

Because of the way in which "Attacks on linking" is written, and because it is just one part of a series of papers on psychosis, Bion's argument is more suggestive than conclusive. The richness of the papers included in this volume testifies not only to how deeply the paper probes but also to how incomplete it is. I would, however, single out one central idea that Bion developed here and in his other papers in the series that, while itself not unambiguous, has profoundly influenced psychoanalytic thinking throughout the world.

Foreshadowed in Freud's view that "Hate as a relation to objects is older than love" (1915c, p. 139) and elaborated in his papers on neurosis and psychosis (1924b,e) Freud believed that contact with reality can, for some people under some conditions, be so unbearably painful that the contact itself must be broken off. However, working with a conceptual structure anchored in repression and related defence mechanisms, Freud was not able even to fully describe the annihilation of reality that characterises psychotic experience.

This is where Bion took Freud more than a step forward. He argued that the dread and hatred of reality leads not only to attacks on the external world and the objects contained within it, but also on our capacity to experience reality at all. Thus, the psychotic (and the psychotic core in all of us) attacks the capacities to think, to feel, and to love because each of these links us to what is feared and loathed. We annihilate our ability to experience itself, because this is seen as what caused the problem in the first place.

The new focus has led to a sea change in clinical work to what has been characterised as a shift from retrieval of repressed or otherwise disavowed mental contents to the repair of damaged or undeveloped capacities. In this volume, for example, Elias and Elizabeth da Rocha Barros elegantly describe the importance of focusing on patients' attacks, not only on symbols, but on symbolic capacity itself. Both the attacks and the terrors to which they lead are vividly illustrated in Edna O'Shaughnessy's account of her work with a child patient.

Because its influence has been so widespread, "Attacks on linking" must be revisited periodically with two questions in mind: where did it come from and—equally importantly—where is it going? The two questions, both controversial and both explored interestingly in the papers collected here, are closely related. Freud (1899a) said early on that the personal histories that we create and live by are decisively shaped by the wishes and needs that lead us to create them in the first place, and the same is true of our histories of psychoanalytic ideas. It is an important contribution of this volume that very different accounts of both the origin and the future of Bion's paper are spelled out with force and clarity.

The contrast emerges clearly in the papers of Rachel Blass and Antonino Ferro; reviewing this briefly will highlight both the ambiguity of Bion's formulations and the potential inherent in them. Ferro claims that the original (1959) version of "Attacks on linking" captures a moment in which Bion is undergoing "a catastrophic change from theories that are his own and that give him peace of mind to theories under development that torment him". In this view, what happens next is bound to shatter what has come before. Blass sees things very differently; she emphasises continuity rather than rupture in Bion's views, a perspective captured in her title "Bion as a Kleinian". We might anticipate that Blass's application of the ideas in the paper will remain more within a traditional framework. Vermote's reading occupies what strikes me as a middle ground between Blass's and Ferro's; he sees the paper as still conservative but is critical of Bion for holding on to what he considers "Kleinian preconceptions".

The differing accounts of the paper's provenance follow from different hopes about how it will be used in the future, both theoretically and clinically. Theoretically, Blass's Kleinian Bion understands "attacks on linking" as destructive phantasies that express wishes to damage the mind itself; the phantasies are driven by what he thought of as the psychotic's over-endowment with aggression. Clinically, this means that the analyst's role—as prescribed by both Freud and Klein—is to interpret the phantasies; Bion's paper does not change much about our understanding of the psychoanalytic situation or about its therapeutic action.

Things are very different for Ferro, who (in considerable agreement with Nemas) reads a paper that foreshadows his own field theoretical approach. For Ferro, Bion's torment stemmed from his dawning recognition of the influence of the "other"—understood as container, mother, analyst, and so on—in the dynamics of the attacks that he described. Consequently, Ferro is little interested in the intrapsychic phantasies that, for Blass, define what psychoanalysts should be attending to. In his view, the "attacks on linking" are comments on the analytic field and—pointedly—on the participation of the analyst. Developing Bion's suggestion that attacks on linking can be communicative rather than simply destructive, Ferro believes that they originate as responses to early experiences of having been denied the use of projective identification. These experiences are repeated—*not* in phantasy but as interpersonal realities—in the consulting room. The "culprit" is "the analyst himself, whose mind may not be sufficiently receptive of . . . projective identifications". The cause of this is "a sort of mental vaginismus *in the other*, or . . . an occlusion through excessive anxiety already present *in the other's mind*" (my emphasis).

Primary destructiveness (borrowed from Freud but surely what Vermote would call a "Kleinian preconception) fades as a dynamic force in this formulation, replaced by occlusions in the field. Interestingly, the analyst's preoccupation with received theory can play a causal role in the analyst's failure to be adequately receptive. The clinical implications are profound, as Ferro's re-analyses of Bion's clinical vignettes illustrates.

As with the dispute about provenance, there is a kind of middle ground in this debate. Britton, like Ferro (and also akin to Vermote) places the "other" in the foreground; it is the other and not just the patient's mind that is the problem in his view. But, for Britton, it is not the object's failure that occupies centre stage; rather, it is what he characterises as the patient's allergic reaction to otherness. Reflecting his middle ground position, Britton prefers to characterise the break with reality (and with those psychic capacities that make reality relations possible) as "disconnection" rather than "attack", thus leaving open the motivating force behind it. This also directs the analyst's attention clinically: Britton concludes that "the patient's fear that free association and acknowledgement of transference love would lead to madness needs to be exposed repeatedly".

Blass, Ferro, Britton, and Vermote are all deeply committed to their readings of "Attacks on linking". Each author, being deeply steeped in Bion's thought as well as being passionate about it, cites chapter and verse from the original texts to prove their point. It is both inspiring and vexing to bear in mind that one paper can be read in such different ways, but more important is that each of these readings leads to such different ways of working and of understanding the work we do. It is remarkable that, in just a few pages, Bion manages to engage virtually every issue that is central to contemporary psychoanalytic discourse, often seeming to offer support to advocates of incompatible points of view. To summarise: among many other themes, he weighs in on the aetiological influence of phantasy and interpersonal experience, the centrality of interpretation in therapeutic action, the role of innate destructiveness and environmental failure in the constitution of object relations and of psychic capacities, and he hints at the analyst's role in shaping the course of treatment.

"Attacks on linking" does raise one issue that cries out for discussion but that, for one reason or another, Bion chooses not to engage. The violence of the attacks he is describing, the catastrophes embodied in the unbearable emotional storms that his analysands experience, are bound to affect any analyst who ventures to work with the kind of patients he describes, or who dare to explore the chaotic depths that can be found in all of us. It is impossible to read "Attacks on linking" without wondering about countertransference; consider, for example, the chaos we feel as we read his very brief clinical vignettes. And although as Bronstein mentions in her Introduction, Bion did take up the issue elsewhere, nothing in the paper addresses the questions that inevitably come to mind. Fortunately, several of the authors in this volume highlight the inevitable countertransferential reverberations of the attacks that Bion describes. Their perspective highlights the value of revisiting seminal papers after many decades; authors viewing the ideas from the perspective of a transformed theory see clearly what could have at best been implicit when the paper was first written.

Consider Horovitz's comment that "Being subjected to such a heavy burden in the transference passion is extenuating. The countertransference is on the front line here". Similarly, Nemas notes that "The degree of pessimism, despair, and devastation that A brought to the sessions led me constantly to try to rescue myself so as not to stay trapped in the apocalyptic world proposed by the patient". Anzieu-Premmereur, who emphasises more than most of the authors that the analysand's attacks are directed at the object (the analyst) as well as at the patient's own mind, echoes this position. Each of these authors skillfully employs Bion's ideas to help navigate through the dangers of engaging patients who are committed to attacking their connections to the object world.

Finally, as with all the themes that we can find in Bion's paper, there is another way of thinking about the relationship between the patient's attacks and the analyst's countertransference. I have noted that the attacks are certain to evoke strong reactions in the analyst, but, for at least two of the authors, the reverse is also true; that is, the analyst's countertransference provokes the attacks. Anzieu-Premmereur is quite explicit about this, arguing that "attacks are reactions to a countertransference that prevented the analyst from being receptive to the projections, insensitive to the emotions in the relationship". Ferro's concept of the analyst's "mental vaginismus" points in the same direction.

Two very different ways of thinking about our work with these difficult patients, and with all patients, both of which are vital for us to think about, thinking that will be stimulated and facilitated by reading and re-reading Bion's remarkable paper and these outstanding commentaries on it.

References

Freud, S. (1899a). Screen memories. *S. E., 3*: 301–322. London: Hogarth.

Freud, S. (1915c). Instincts and their vicissitudes. *S. E., 14*: 111–140. London: Hogarth.

Freud, S. (1924b). Neurosis and psychosis. *S. E., 19*: 149–155. London: Hogarth.

Freud, S. (1924e). The loss of reality in neurosis and psychosis. *S. E., 19*: 183–190. London: Hogarth.

Introduction

Catalina Bronstein

Wilfred Bion's contributions are a continuous source of psychoanalytic inspiration. The originality of his investigations into the workings of the mind and its functions have opened up an enormous variety of avenues for exploration. Bion's interest in group work, in developing a theory of knowledge, in philosophy and language, as well as his acute insight into psychotic states of mind, paved the way for developments that are far from exhausted. This book aims at providing further contributions inspired by his paper "Attacks on linking" (1959) by a distinguished group of scholars who have focused on different aspects of Bion's propositions. We chose to publish here the version of "Attacks on linking" that appeared in Bion's compilation, *Second Thoughts*, as this includes the commentary added in 1967.

The papers on psychosis written between 1950 and 1962, and later rounded up in *Second Thoughts* (1967a), brought new ideas to the understanding of psychosis, but, more importantly, they laid the foundations for Bion's theory of thinking. Bion followed many of Freud and Klein's ideas in this area, though he always imbued them with his own. It would be impossible to mention all the different and relevant influences on Bion's work. He was well versed in history, philosophy, mathematics, literature, psychiatry, and, of course, psychoanalysis. At the time he was writing "Attacks on linking", he was reading Braithwaite's *Scientific Explanation: A Study of the Function of Theory, Probability and Law in Science* (1946) (Britton, 2016) and, as Bion mentions in his "Commentary" in *Second Thoughts*, he was also influenced by Heisenberg's *Physics and Philosophy* (1958). However, I would like to mention here the impact that some specific psychoanalytic ideas and papers had on his work. One of them was Freud's "Formulations on the two principles of mental functioning" (1911b), where he reflects on the origins of thought and the connection between the restraint of motor discharge and the development of the process of thinking. In this paper, Freud also proposes the idea that thinking originates in the unconscious, that it "went beyond mere ideational presentations and was directed to the relations between impressions of objects, and that it did not acquire further qualities perceptible to consciousness, until it became connected with verbal residues" (1911b, p. 221).

Freud's distinction between the pleasure principle and the reality principle was central to Bion's thinking. Freud's paper on "Neurosis and psychosis" (1924b), with its emphasis on the reality principle, the psychotic's hatred of reality, and the development of verbal thought, is another paper that he seems to have drawn on. Bion himself mentioned the impact that the *Interpretation of Dreams* (1900a), his *New Introductory Lectures on Psycho-Analysis* (1933a), and "Instincts and their vicissitudes" (1915c) had on his work (1992, p. 62). Bion was particularly interested in the patient's attitude towards reality and the distinction between measures to evade and modify reality. I would like to stress here that "reality" includes both external as well as internal reality. Sometimes, the denial of external reality is a correlate of the inability to tolerate psychic reality (Bion, 1967b[1950]; Bléandonu, 1994). In Chapter Seven, Horovitz presents us with an example where the hatred of internal and external reality is effected through an attack on the setting which, as she elegantly describes, is the space of resonance and signification that enables the analyst to hear and "to bring into existence what one hears, the plurality of the links gives flesh to speech". She also adds an interesting point: that the discontinuity of linking is absolutely necessary as it permits separation and triangulation.

Bion saw the relationship between object-impressions as a primitive matrix of ideographs from which thought springs, and that contains within itself links between one ideograph and another

(1967e[1957]). In *Cogitations* (1992), Bion differentiated experiences that appear to be transformed by alpha function from those that cannot be transformed. In order for a sense impression to be transformed by alpha function, the impression must stay for some length of time (it has to acquire some durability) and must be ideogrammaticised. Bion gave the example that if the experience is of pain, the psyche must have some visual image of "rubbing an elbow, or a tearful face". He added,

> If the reality principle is dominant, then the object of the ideogram will be to make the experience suitable for storage and recall; if the pleasure–pain principle is dominant, the tendency will be to have as the object of the ideogram its value as an excretable object. (1992, p. 64)

In this book, in Chapter Five, Elias and Elizabeth da Rocha Barros explore these early forms of mental representations of emotional experiences, or "affective pictograms", that can subsequently be used for the creation of thoughts. These authors have written about the role of symbolism in sustaining other mental functions by exploring both its representative and expressive qualities. They have explored how the association between the evolution of symbolic processes as described by Langer (1942) and Bion's concept of "transformations" provide a key to understanding the mode of operation of symbolic forms and the way they can be attacked and mutilated (da Rocha Barros & da Rocha Barros, 2015). Destructive impulses invade the process of symbolic construction (da Rocha Barros & da Rocha Barros, 2011). Through the interpretation of a patient's dream, they illustrate their idea that images are "kernels of meaning", first symbolic forms that "exist virtually in the links that are likely to be established if emotional experiences are wakened in the intersubjective experience with the analyst". These can be split and prevented from developing. These authors are in agreement with Ferro's proposition that dream images are part of transforming experiences towards the development of thinkability. The idea of transformation in dreaming and the development of thinkability in the context of the psychoanalytic "field", as proposed by the Barangers (1961–1962), is explored by Ferro in Chapter Nine, "Attacks on linking, or uncontainability of beta elements?"

Symbolic impairment is also addressed by O'Shaughnessy in Chapter Eight, "Turning away to Frankenstein". She describes a boy,

Hugh, for whom words were often symbolic equations. O'Shaughnessy sees this as the consequence of the death drive, leading to the dissolution of the units and the destruction of vitality in Hugh's mind. Thus, his language was unable to contend with new and more complex ideas. Hugh had to resort to "ready mades" in order to express himself. Hugh created a mask of Frankenstein, which made him feel that he actually was Frankenstein. This brought enormous excitement, but at the same time made him frantic as he was still trapped internally with a terrifying persecuting maternal object.

Second Thoughts *(1967)*

Even though each paper in the collection published in *Second Thoughts* contains original ideas, all share common ideas that continue to be developed. Therefore, the notions explored in "Attacks on linking" (1959) could be seen to arise from ideas Bion wrote about in earlier papers.

After his work on theories of group psychology Bion started to write psychoanalytic papers that were aimed more specifically at understanding the individual's psyche. However, his understanding of group psychology continued to have an important effect on his later ideas. One of the propositions that seem relevant to his later developments is that when people come together as a group there is a creation of "basic assumptions". The "basic assumption group", such as the dependence, pairing, and flight/fight group, does not recognise the passage of time. Conflict arises from the relation between the basic assumption groups and the rational work group (Bion, 1961; Bléandonu, 1994). Bion used the term "valency", which he borrowed from physicists, to describe individuals' capacity for "involuntary combination of one individual with another for sharing and acting on a basic assumption" (1952, p. 235). He thought this was the spontaneous and unconscious function of the gregarious quality of our personality. The different ways in which people can combine and link to each other was one of Bion's early preoccupations, one that I think contributed to his development of the notion of projective identification as communication.

Another important early concept relevant to his later writings is that of the "proto-mental system" which he defined as a matrix, "in which physical and psychological or mental are undifferentiated . . . It is from this matrix that emotions proper to the basic assumption flow to reinforce, pervade, and, on occasion, to dominate the mental life of the group" (1961, p. 102). Bion suggested that basic assumptions can emerge "as formations secondary to an extremely early primal scene worked out on a level of part objects, and associated with psychotic anxiety and projective identification such as Melanie Klein has described" (1961, p. 164). He saw this version of the primal scene as a link between part-objects where "parts of one parent, the breast or the mother's body, contains among other objects a part of the father" (1961, p. 164). This is a subject he returned to in "Attacks on linking". He believed that projective identification involves an omnipotent phantasy that changes the relationship subject–object into subject–subject (bringing fusion instead of connection), which Britton discusses in the first chapter of this book.

Bion's papers on psychosis, published between 1950 and 1962, are still immensely helpful to our understanding of psychotic processes. But more than this, they are highly illuminating as to the workings of impulses and defences, of projective identification and unconscious phantasies, of transference and countertransference, and the relationship between thought and language. I will try to summarise some of the findings described in these earlier papers that I think had some influence on "Attacks on linking".

In "The imaginary twin" (1967b[1950]), Bion described the use of an imaginary twin to deny reality as an expression of the inability to tolerate an object that is not under the patient's control. The denial of external reality co-exists with an inability to tolerate psychic reality. We can here see Bion's interest on the causes and effects carried out by split-off parts of the personality. He proposed the idea of a particular link between ocular development, the development of intellect, and the Oedipus complex. Bion arrived at the thought that,

> in each case I had the impression that the patient felt that sight produced problems of mastery of a new sense organ. This had its counterpart in a feeling that development of the psyche, like development of visual capacity, involved the emergence of the Oedipus Complex. (1967b[1950], p. 21)

Bion considered this a manifestation of the coming together of physical and emotional development, which, for him, was evidence of the correctness of Klein's view of an early oedipal phase. The relevance of the oedipal predicament on the subject's attack on his mental functioning occupies a central place in Bion's thinking.

In his commentary on "The imaginary twin" that he made in *Second Thoughts*, he remarked on a subject to which he returned many times, that of an "ineffable experience", one that cannot be sensuously grasped (1967b, p. 121). We see here the importance he attributes to the splitting of the ego and objects, and to projective identification due to the influence of heightened destructive impulses (1967b[1950]). Bion also made extensive use of the concept of countertransference, which he contributed to expanding (Meltzer, 1978).

In "Notes on the theory of schizophrenia" (1967c[1953]) we can see a number of propositions that had an impact on further developments, such as his belief that the outstanding feature of schizophrenia is the peculiarity of the schizophrenic's object relations. He discussed three ways in which the schizophrenic uses language (as a mode of action, as a method of communication, and as a mode of thought). This mode of thought is frequently omnipotent and is predominantly in the service either of splitting the object or projective identification. He also described how attacks on verbal thought are connected to attacks on the awareness of psychic reality, and of the depression linked to the destruction of the good object. Bion proposed that destructive attacks are greatly aimed against parental intercourse "whether sexual or verbal" (1967c[1953], p. 30). It is worth stressing the importance he placed on attacks on the reality of parental intercourse.

Bion's later paper, "Developments of schizophrenic thought" (1967d[1956]), continued to highlight the role that hatred of reality, both external and internal, has, and he proposed that it could lead to a dread of annihilation. He remarked on the impact of the conflict between the life and death drives and discussed in greater detail the role that projective identification has in the psychotic personality, in the sense that it constitutes an attempt to rid the self of the apparatus of conscious awareness of internal and external reality. The patient's sense of being imprisoned in his state of mind, having in phantasy expelled parts of his ego, and left with a failure in his capacity for perception, is extremely helpful for the understanding of psychotic phenomena. The role of the drives, the preponderance of destructive impulses, the hatred of both internal and external reality, and the use of minute splitting and expulsion of the fragments of the apparatus of awareness of reality is explored in greater detail in "Differentiation of the psychotic from the non-psychotic personalities" (1967e[1957]). While this withdrawal of reality is an illusion that is based on an omnipotent unconscious phantasy, the contact with reality is maintained thanks to the non-psychotic personality. The main role of projective identification in this paper is seen to be the expulsion of fragments of the personality into external objects, leading to the possibility of being surrounded by bizarre objects. There is an indication here of some of the ideas that Bion continued to develop in "Attacks on linking". He states that,

> not only is primitive thought attacked because it links sense-impressions of reality with consciousness but, thanks to the psychotic's over-endowment with destructiveness, the splitting processes are extended to the links within the thought processes themselves . . . [the] primitive matrix of ideographs from which thought springs contains within itself links between one ideograph and other. (1967e[1957], p. 50)

If these links are attacked, then the formation of symbols becomes very difficult. Later, the result of these attacks can be seen in difficulties with combining words and, even further,

> since that-which-links has been not only minutely fragmented but also projected out into objects to join the other bizarre objects, the patient feels surrounded by minute links, which being impregnated now with cruelty, link objects together cruelly. (1967e[1957], p. 50)

I have quoted these passages to show Bion's evolving interest in the notion of "attacks on linking" in conjunction with the development of the capacity to think.

At the end of his paper "On arrogance", Bion states,

> In some patients the denial to the patient of a normal employment of projective identification precipitates a disaster through the destruction of an important link. Inherent in this disaster is the establishment of a primitive superego which denies the use of projective identification. (1967e[1957], p. 92)

With this statement, Bion paved the way to the development of a new view of Klein's projective identification, which he expanded in

"Attacks on linking" in the section headed "Denial of normal degrees of projective identification", and continued to develop in *Learning from Experience* through his idea of container–contained and reverie (1962). I think it is worth highlighting his idea of the destructive role a primitive superego has in the development of the personality by interfering with the establishment of a nurturing communication with the object. There is a connection between a pathological superego and failures in communication between infant and mother. As O'Shaughnessy has described, this can be relived in the transference and can lead to a situation where patient and analyst relate as "abnormal superego to abnormal superego" (1999). I think this also lies at the root of analytic situations where there is a prevalent feeling of deep disappointment (Bronstein, 2015)

Bion's 1962 paper, "A theory of thinking" (1967g), continued to develop these contributions into a highly creative theory of the mind centred on the idea of the development of thoughts as requiring an apparatus to cope with them. The concepts of alpha function and maternal reverie are also explored here.

"Attacks on linking" (1959) and the role of projective identification

Bion stated that "Attacks on linking" was an expansion of his previous paper, "Differentiation of the psychotic from the non-psychotic personalities" (1967e[1957]). However, he also brought novel ideas while continuing to develop what he had previously expressed. This paper paved the way for his 1962 paper, "A theory of thinking" (1967g) and his later book, *Learning from Experience* (1962).

Bion's seminal idea that the patient might make "destructive attacks . . . on anything which is felt to have the function of linking one object with another" is of great clinical help, as it makes us aware of the need to take into account the dynamic field and all of the forces and phantasies that come to life within it. As Bion proposed, the prototype for all links is "the primitive breast or penis", but we should use this notion as just a prototype. We can encounter many other objects as well as functions that play this role. Following this, I think another seminal idea proposed by Bion is that the attack is not necessarily aimed at the *object* (the breast) but at the *function*, "not with anatomy but with physiology" (Bion, 1967e[1957]; Bronstein, 2001).

Bion expanded our understanding of the mechanism of projective identification. He recognised his debt to Melanie Klein's notions of the "paranoid" and "depressive positions", adding that "Melanie Klein's work occupies a central position in my view of the psychoanalytic theory of schizophrenia" (1967c[1953], p. 23). "Attacks on linking" came after Klein's paper, "Notes on some schizoid mechanisms" (1980[1946]), where she discusses projective identification within the context of scientific exchanges with Hanna Segal and Herbert Rosenfeld, who, at that time, were writing about their own work with psychotic patients. In Chapter Three, Rachel Blass provides an interesting study of the connection between Klein and Bion's concepts of unconscious phantasy and projective identification. She proposes that one of Bion's major contributions is that the central phantasy expressed in "Attacks on linking", rather than being a phantasy of objects that constitute the mind, is the phantasy of the mind itself. This phantasy of the mind centres on one major image, which is the mind as a connecting force. She sees this development as one that is embedded in the Kleinian tradition. A different point of view is introduced by Vermote in Chapter Four, who describes projective identification not just at the level of phantasy, but stresses that something is really passing over from the patient to the analyst. The omnipotent phantasy could be seen as a defence against the attacks of an "obstructive object" (a kind of cruel, primitive superego) such as the one that Bion highlights in his paper "On arrogance" (1967f[1957]).

Klein employed the term "projective identification" to describe a particular form of identification "which establishes the prototype of an aggressive object-relation" based on the infant's unconscious phantasy of evacuating bad parts of the self (such as excrements and split parts of the ego) into the mother (Bell, 2001; Klein, 1980[1946]). O'Shaughnessy's (2015) chapter clearly illustrates this aspect by showing how her patient, Hugh, projected aspects of himself into the "ready made" Frankenstein mask as an attempt to escape from the reality of the murderous figure in his internal world (and, perhaps, the mother in the external world too) and also from the unbearable pain of his deprivation.

While, for Bion, projective identification is here described as the "mechanism employed by the psyche to dispose of the ego fragments produced by its destructiveness" (Bion, 1959, p. 93), he anticipates what will later become his model of container–contained, that is, the idea that the infant's projective identification is an early method of preverbal communication with the mother and necessary for the development of thoughts. As Riesenberg-Malcolm (2001) explains, projective identification is the central and "most primary link between infant and mother and the capacity to use it, transform it and assimilate it forms the core for both normal and pathological development" (p. 165). These two uses leave us with the need to make a distinction between normal and pathological forms of projective identification (Spillius, 2012). This is, of course, not easy to assess, but, according to Bion, development seems to rest on a "normal degree of projective identification" that is associated and combined with introjective identification (1959, p. 103).

Bion will later explore both the consequences of the object's unreceptiveness to the infant's projections as well as those damaging attacks on projective identification that stem from the infant and patients. The understanding of the role of the object in his/her capacity to receive projections, to accept them and appropriately respond to them, is of great clinical value and has significantly advanced our thinking on psychoanalytic technique in connection to patients' reactions to our interpretations (Bronstein, 2014). Ferro has underlined the relevance of Bion's contribution to the understanding of the process of thinking and the process of dreaming (2011). In Chapter Nine, he suggests that, instead of an attack on linking, we should think of an attack on the capacities for projective identification. The subject of the role of projective identification in connection to attacks on linking and the effects it has on the development of a capacity to think has been, and continue to be, of great interest both to analysts who follow the Kleinian tradition and those from other schools of thought.

The interpersonal effect of parental destructiveness on the child is presented in a clear and evocative way by Christine Anzieu-Premmereur in Chapter Six. She addresses how psychotic projections from parents interfere with the child's capacity for symbolisation. In her work as a child psychoanalyst with parents and their infants, Anzieu-Premmereur sees the parent's attacks as their reaction to a countertransference that prevents the analyst from being receptive to their projections. She explores the early development of the superego and paradoxical situations in which the superego becomes confused with the ego-ideal, and shows that the use of paradoxical communications in parents leads to an increase in splitting and difficulties for the child developing appropriate ego boundaries. Anzieu-Premmereur highlights the fundamental importance of the analytic function of containment and reverie when working with the parents' powerful countertransferences.

The notion of "catastrophe" appears frequently in Bion's writing. Some of the papers in *Second Thoughts* postulate the notion of a psychic "catastrophe". Bion thought that "verbal thought is so interwoven with catastrophe and the painful emotion of depression that the patient, resorting to projective identification, splits it off and pushes it into the analyst" (1967c[1953], p. 32). For example, in his later work *Elements of Psycho-Analysis* (1963) he wrote that *B*-elements are objects "compounded of things-in-themselves, feelings of depression and guilt and therefore aspects of personality linked by a sense of catastrophe" (p. 40). In "Attacks on linking", we are reminded of a catastrophe that remains vital and yet is incapable of being resolved. The cause of this catastrophe is partly explained by Bion in "On arrogance" as stemming from the "mutilating attacks made upon this extremely primitive species of link between the patient and the analyst" (1957, p. 92). The "primitive" link that is being attacked is projective identification. Perhaps the main issue here is that Bion uses "the theory of projective identification as a model for the early development of processes that have come later to be known as thinking" (2016[1961]). This is discussed in connection to the patient's fear of death that needed to be contained by the analyst so that, as Bion says, "[it] would undergo modification by my psyche and could then be safely introjected" (Bion, 1959, p. 103). According to Alvarez (1998), Bion has two seemingly different positions regarding failures in linking: one that refers to the effect of destructive attacks on the patient's own thinking and the other to the idea of a deficit in linking. Do all incapacities to think derive from attacks on links or can we also assume a deficit in this capacity? (Alvarez, 1998).

In Chapter Four, Vermote highlights the relationship between catastrophe and a primary traumatic problem with the accent being placed on the failure of normal projective identification with the mother or carer. Ferro also comments on this in Chapter Nine. He reminds us that Bion thought that the catastrophe can shift at the very moment it is being studied. He suggests helpfully that "in the face of the catastrophe, we cannot ask ourselves 'Why did it happen?' but only 'In what does it consist?'" Bion's notion of catastrophe will later acquire other dimensions when he describes the role that catastrophic change has in analysis. In Chapter Seven, Horovitz brings an evocative clinical example of a patient's catastrophic experience of his emergent violence with the reactivation of the effects of an earlier trauma after the analyst had to defer some sessions. Her writing reminds us of the economic factor, where the prevalence of unbinding has a powerful effect on the transference–countertransference as it is lived out in the analytic situation, and great impact on the setting.

We could extend Bion's propositions in order to understand the notion of dissociation in psychosis, and the role it has in the eradication of the awareness of the coming together of aspects of the self.

Britton's chapter highlights the "psychotic urge to disconnect arising from psychic allergy to foreign objects and the 'perceptions they give rise to'". He describes how, through the elimination of the psychic representation of an object, the subject can eradicate the awareness of the object. Thus, "the actual link, the sensory connection to an object, would be wiped out" with no possibility for introjection. Through examples based both on literature, such as Blake's poetry, and clinical cases, Britton shows us how the employment of violence leads to the feeling that it is not just the object that is felt to disintegrate but also the mental apparatus of the person carrying out the attack. He discusses the psychotic "solution of dis-connection" in relation to the concept of "primary narcissism" which, in these cases, he sees as a reaction and the consequence of the "abolition of object relations".

In Chapter Two, Clara Nemas highlights the role of envy in attacks on linking, when one of the main problems an infant faces is the generosity of the good object. Her clinical example puts us in touch with her patient's manipulation and attacks on her body that Nemas sees arising as the result of her need to deny her origin in the intercourse of the parents. Her patient's conflict with accepting the dependence on the breast and the reality of the parental intercourse that created her, with the subsequent attacks on linking, are exemplified through the patient's manipulation of her body, necessary as a proof of being her own creation, of a "phantasy of auto gestation". Nemas also stresses the consequences for our technique, as we need to be aware that "it is the realisation of the fragility of the link that needs to be protected from both members of the couple".

Vermote helpfully discusses the ideas stemming from "Attacks on linking" in Chapter Four. He sees these as belonging to Bion's notion of transformations in K (thinking, making experiences psychic) in contrast to the notion of transformations in O, where Bion saw rational understanding as a hindrance to "seeing or intuiting conjunctions and patterns". Vermote proposes an evolution in Bion to a model of different layers of psychic functioning and examines Bion's examples from different angles informed by both his early and late work. "Attacks on linking" is a ground-breaking paper that not only illuminates the individual's personal struggle, but can also help us understand social phenomena. As Clara Nemas writes, "what is the place for emotional links in our society nowadays?"

I hope that this book contributes to the development of psychoanalysis by being an example of "research into the domain of the mind itself, an expedition" (Bion, 1968, p. 62).

References

Alvarez, A. (1998). Failures to link: attacks or defects? Some questions concerning the thinkability of oedipal and pre-oedipal thoughts. *Journal of Child Psychotherapy, 24*: 213–231.

Baranger, M., & Baranger, W. (1961–1962). La situación analitica como campo dinamico. *Revista Uruguaya de Psicoanalisis, 5*: 1–14.

Bell, D. (2001). Projective identification. In: C. Bronstein (Ed.), *Kleinian Theory. A Contemporary Perspective* (pp. 125–156). London: Wiley.

Bion, W. R. (1952). Group dynamics: a re-view. *International Journal of Psychoanalysis, 33*: 235–247.

Bion, W. R. (1959). Attacks on linking. In: *Second Thoughts* (pp. 93–109). New York: Jason Aronson.

Bion, W. R. (1961). *Experiences in Groups and Other Papers.* London: Tavistock.

Bion, W. R. (1962). *Learning from Experience.* London: Karnac [reprinted 1991].

Bion, W. R. (1963). *Elements of Psycho-Analysis.* London: Heinemann.

Bion, W. R. (1967a). *Second Thoughts.* New York: Jason Aronson.

Bion, W. R. (1967b)[1950]. The imaginary twin. In: *Second Thoughts* (pp. 3–22). New York: Jason Aronson.

Bion, W. R. (1967c)[1953]. Notes on the theory of schizophrenia. In: *Second Thoughts* (pp. 23–35). New York: Jason Aronson.

Bion, W. R. (1967d)[1956]. Development of schizophrenic thought. In: *Second Thoughts* (pp. 36–42). New York: Jason Aronson.

Bion, W. R. (1967e)[1957]. Differentiation of the psychotic from the non-psychotic personalities. In: *Second Thoughts* (pp. 43–64). New York: Jason Aronson.

Bion, W. R. (1967f)[1957]. On arrogance. In: *Second Thoughts. Selected Papers on Psycho-Analysis* (pp. 86–92). New York: Jason Aronson.

Bion, W. R. (1967g)[1962]. A theory of thinking. In: *Second Thoughts* (pp. 110–119). New York: Jason Aronson.

Bion, W. R. (1968). *The Complete Works of W. R. Bion, Vol. XV*. C. Mawson (Ed). London: Karnac, 2014.

Bion, W. R. (1992). *Cogitations*. London: Karnac.

Bion, W. R. (2016)[1961]. The conception of man. In: C. Mawson (Ed.), *The Complete Works of W. R. Bion* (pp. 10–29). London: Karnac.

Bléandonu, G. (1994). *Wilfred Bion. His Life and Works, 1897–1979*. London: Free Association Books.

Braithwaite, R. B. (1946). *Scientific Explanation: A Study of the Function of Theory, Probability and Law in Science*. Cambridge: Cambridge University Press.

Britton, R. (2016). Non-analytic influences on the psychoanalytic theorising of Wilfred Bion. In: H. Levine & G. Civitarese (Eds.), *The W. R. Bion Tradition* (pp. 29–38). London: Karnac.

Bronstein, C. (2001). What are internal objects? In: C. Bronstein (Ed.), *Kleinian Theory. A Contemporary Perspective* (pp. 108–124). London: Wiley.

Bronstein, C. (2014). 'I am not crying. I am rubbing my eyes': Annie and the hollow object. *Journal of Child Psychotherapy, 40*: 135–149.

Bronstein, C. (2015). The analyst's disappointment: an everyday struggle. *Journal of the American Psychoanalytic Association, 63*: 1173–1192.

Da Rocha Barros, E. M., & Da Rocha Barros, E. L. (2011). Reflections on the clinical implications of symbolism. *International Journal of Psychoanalysis, 92*(4): 879–901.

Da Rocha Barros, E. M., & Da Rocha Barros, E. L. (2015). Symbolism, emotions and mental growth. In: J. Borossa, C. Bronstein, & C. Pajaczkowska (Eds.), *The New Klein–Lacan Dialogues* (pp. 235–255). London: Karnac.

Ferro, A. (2011). Shuttles to and from the unconscious: reveries, transformations in dreaming, and dreams. *Italian Psychoanalytic Annual, 5*: 89–105

Freud, S. (1900a). *The Interpretation of Dreams. S. E., 4–5*. London: Hogarth.

Freud, S. (1911b). Formulations on the two principles of mental functioning. *S. E., 12*: 215–226. London: Hogarth.

Freud, S. (1915c). Instincts and their vicissitudes. *S. E., 14*: 111–140. London: Hogarth.
Freud, S. (1924b[1923]). Neurosis and psychosis. *S. E., 19*: 149–153. London: Hogarth.
Freud, S. (1933a). *New Introductory Lectures in Psycho-Analysis. S. E.,* 22. London: Hogarth.
Heisenberg, W. (1958). *Physics and Philosophy*. London: Allen and Unwin.
Klein, M. (1980)[1946]. Notes on some schizoid mechanisms. In: *Envy and Gratitude and Other Works* (pp. 1–24). London: Hogarth Press.
Langer, S. K. (1942). *Philosophy in a New Key: A Study in the Symbolism of Reason, Rite and Art.* Cambridge, MA: Harvard University Press.
Meltzer, D. (1978). *The Kleinian Development. Part III. The Clinical Significance of the World of Bion.* Strathtay, Perthshire: Clunie Press.
O'Shaughnessy, E. (1999). Relating to the superego. *International Journal of Psychoanalysis, 80*: 861–870.
O'Shaughnessy, E. (Ed.) (2015). A projective identification with Frankenstein: some questions about psychic limits. In: *Inquires in Psychoanalysis* (pp. 201–214). London: Routledge.
Riesenberg-Malcolm, R. (2001). Bion's theory of containment. In: C. Bronstein (Ed.), *Kleinian Theory. A Contemporary Perspective* (pp. 165–180). London: Wiley.
Spillius, E. (2012). Developments by British Kleinian analysts. In: E. Spillius & E. O'Shaughnessy (Eds.), *Projective Identification. The Fate of a Concept* (pp. 49–60). London: The New Library of Psychoanalysis.

Original Papers

Attacks on linking

W. R. Bion

92. In a previous paper [chapter 5] I have had occasion, in talking of the psychotic part of the personality, to speak of the destructive attacks which the patient makes on anything which is felt to have the function of linking one object with another. It is my intention in this paper to show the significance of this form of destructive attack in the production of some symptoms met with in borderline psychosis.

The prototype for all the links of which I wish to speak is the primitive breast or penis. The paper presupposes familiarity with Melanie Klein's descriptions of the infant's fantasies of sadistic attacks upon the breast (Klein, 1935); of the infant's splitting of its objects; of projective identification—which is the name she gives to the mechanism by which parts of the personality are split off and projected into external objects—and finally, her views on early stages of Oedipus complex (Klein, 1928). I shall discuss phantasied attacks on the breast as the prototype of all attacks on objects that serve as a link, and projective identification as the mechanism employed by the psyche to dispose of the ego fragments produced by its destructiveness.

I shall first describe clinical manifestations in an order dictated not by the chronology of their appearance in the consulting room, but by the need for making the exposition of my thesis as clear as I can. I shall follow this with material selected to demonstrate the order which these mechanisms assume when their relationship to each other is determined by the dynamics of the analytic situation. I shall conclude with theoretical observations on the material presented. The examples are drawn from the analysis of two patients and are taken from an advanced stage of their analyses. To preserve anonymity I shall not distinguish between the patients, and shall introduce distortions of fact which I hope do not impair the accuracy of the analytic description.

Observation of the patient's disposition to attack the link between two objects is simplified because the analyst has to establish a link with the patient and does this by verbal communication and his equipment of psychoanalytic experience. Upon this the creative relationship depends and we should therefore be able to see attacks being made upon it.

I am not concerned with typical resistance to interpretations, but with expanding references [in chapter 5] to the destructive attacks on verbal thought itself.

Clinical examples

93. The following examples describe occasions which afforded me an opportunity to give the patient an interpretation (which at that point he could understand) of conduct designed to destroy whatever it was that linked two objects together.

(i) I gave the patient an interpretation making explicit his feelings of affection and his expression of them to his mother for her ability to cope with a refractory child. He attempted to express his agreement with me, but although he needed to say only a few words his expression of them was interrupted by a very pronounced stammer which had the effect of spreading out his remark over a period of as much as a minute and a half. The actual sounds emitted bore resemblance to gasping for breath; gaspings were interspersed with gurgling sounds as if he were immersed in water. I drew his attention to these sounds and he agreed that they were peculiar, and suggesting the descriptions I have just given.

(ii) The patient complained that he could not sleep. Showing signs of fear, lie said, "It can't go on like this". Disjointed remarks gave the impression that he felt superficially that some catastrophe would occur, perhaps akin to insanity, if he could not get more sleep. Referring to material in the previous session I suggested that he feared he would dream if he were to sleep. He denied this and said he could not think because he was wet. I reminded him of his use of the term "wet" as an expression of contempt for somebody he regarded as feeble and sentimental. He disagreed and indicated that the state to which he referred was the exact opposite. From what I knew of this patient I felt that his correction at this point was valid, and that somehow the wetness referred to an expression of hatred and envy such as he associated with urinary attacks on an object. I therefore said that in addition to the superficial fear which he had expressed, he was afraid of sleep because for him it was the same thing as the oozing away of his mind itself. Further associations showed that he felt that good interpretations from me were so consistently and minutely split up by him that they became mental urine which then seeped uncontrollably away. Sleep was therefore inseparable from unconsciousness, which was itself identical with a state of mindlessness which could not be repaired. He said, "I am dry now". I replied that he felt he was awake and capable of thought, but that this good state was only precariously maintained.

(iii) In this session the patient had produced material stimulated by the preceding week-end break. His awareness of such external stimuli had become demonstrable at a comparatively recent stage of the analysis. Previously it had been a matter for conjecture how much he was capable of appreciating reality. I knew that he had contact with reality because he came for analysis by himself, but that fact could hardly be deduced from his behaviour in the sessions. When I interpreted some associations as evidence that he felt he had been and still was witnessing an intercourse between two people, he reacted as if he had received a violent blow. I was not then able to say just where he had experienced the assault and even in retrospect I have no clear impression. It would seem logical to suppose that the shock had been administered by my interpretation and that therefore the blow came from without, but my impression is that he felt it as delivered from within; the patient often experienced what he described as a stabbing attack from inside. He sat up and stared intently into space. I said that he seemed to be seeing something. He replied that he could not see what he saw. I was able from previous experience to interpret that he felt he was 'seeing' an invisible object, and subsequent experience convinced me that in the two patients on whose analysis I am depending for material for this paper, events occurred in which the patient experienced invisible–visual hallucinations. I shall give my reasons later for supposing that in this and the previous example similar mechanisms were at work.

(iv) In the first twenty minutes of the session the patient made three isolated remarks which had no significance for me. He then said that it seemed that a girl he had met was understanding. This was followed at once by a violent, convulsive movement which he affected to ignore. It appeared to be identical with the kind of stabbing attack I mentioned in the last example. I tried to draw his attention to the movement, but he had ignored my intervention as he had ignored the attack. He then said that the room was filled with a blue haze. A little later he remarked that the haze had gone, but said he was depressed. I interpreted that he felt understood by me. This was an agreeable experience, but the pleasant feeling of being understood had been instantly destroyed and ejected. I reminded him that we had recently witnessed his use of the word "blue" as a compact description of vituperative sexual conversation. If my interpretation was correct, and subsequent events suggested that it was, it meant that the experience of being understood had been split up, converted into particles of sexual abuse and ejected. Up to this point I felt that the interpretation approximated closely to his experience. Later interpretations, that the disappearance of the haze was due to reintrojection and conversion into depression, seemed to have less reality for the patient, although later events were compatible with its being correct.

(v) This session, like the one in my last example, began with three or four statements of fact, such as that it was hot; that his train was crowded; and that it was Wednesday—this occupied thirty minutes. An impression that he was trying to retain contact with reality was confirmed when he followed up by saying that he feared a breakdown. A little later he said I would not understand him. I interpreted that he felt I was bad and would not take in what he wanted to put into me. I interpreted in these terms deliberately because he had shown in the previous session that he felt that my interpretations were an attempt to eject feelings that he wished to deposit in me. His response to my interpretation was to say that he felt there were two probability clouds in the room. I interpreted that he was trying to get rid of the feeling that my badness was a fact. I said it meant that he needed to know whether I was really bad or whether I was some bad thing which had come from inside him. Although the point was not at that moment of central significance, I thought the patient was attempting to decide whether he was hallucinated or not. This recurrent anxiety in his analysis was associated with his fear that envy and hatred of a capacity for understanding was leading him to take in a good, understanding object in order to destroy and eject it—a procedure which had often led to persecution by the destroyed and ejected object. Whether my refusal to understand was a reality or an hallucination was important only because it determined what painful experiences were to be expected next.

(vi) Half the session passed in silence; the patient then announced that a piece of iron had fallen on the floor. Thereafter he made a series of convulsive movements in silence as if he felt he was being physically assaulted from within. I said he could not establish contact with me because of his fear of what was going on inside him. He confirmed this by saying that he felt he was being murdered. He did not know what he would do without the analysis as it made him better. I said that he felt so envious of himself and of me for being able to work together to make him feel better that he took the pair of us into him as a dead piece of iron and a dead floor that came together not to give him life but to murder him. He became very anxious and said he could not go on. I said that he felt he could not go on because he was either dead, or alive and so envious that he had to stop good analysis. There was a marked decrease of anxiety, but the remainder of the session was taken up by isolated statements of fact which again seemed to be an attempt to preserve contact with external reality as a method of denial of his phantasies.

Features common to the above illustrations

94. These episodes have been chosen by me because the dominant theme in each was the destructive attack on a link. In the first, the attack was expressed in a stammer which was designed to prevent the patient from using language as a bond between him and me. In the second, sleep was felt by him to be identical with projective identification that proceeded unaffected by any possible attempt at control by him. Sleep for him meant that his mind, minutely fragmented, flowed out in an attacking stream of particles.

The examples I give here throw light on schizophrenic dreaming. The psychotic patient appears to have no dreams, or at least not to report any, until comparatively late in the analysis. My impression now is that this apparently dreamless period is a phenomenon analogous to the invisible–visual hallucination. That is to say, the dreams consist of material so minutely fragmented that they are devoid of any visual component. When dreams are experienced which the patient can report because visual objects have been experienced by him in the course of the dream, he seems to regard these objects as bearing much the same relationship to the invisible objects of the previous phase as faeces seem, to him, to bear to urine. The objects appearing in experiences which we call dreams are regarded by the patient as solid and are, as such, contrasted with the contents of the dreams which were a continuum of minute, invisible fragments.

At the time of the session the main theme was not an attack on the link but the consequences of such an attack, previously made, in leaving him bereft of a state of mind necessary for the establishment of a satisfying relationship between him and his bed. Though it did not appear in the session I report, uncontrollable projective identification, which was what sleep meant to him, was thought to be a destructive attack on the state of mind of the coupling parents. There was therefore a double anxiety: one arising from his fear that he was being rendered mindless, the other from his fear that he was unable to control his hostile attacks, his mind providing the ammunition, on the state of mind that was the link between the parental pair. Sleep and sleeplessness were alike unacceptable.

In the third example, in which I described visual hallucinations of invisible objects, we witness one form in which the actual attack on the sexual pair is delivered. My interpretation, as far as I could judge, was felt by him as if it were his own visual sense of a parental intercourse; this visual impression is minutely fragmented and ejected at once in particles so minute that they are the invisible components of a continuum. The total procedure has served the purpose of forestalling an experience of feelings of envy for the parental state of mind by the instantaneous expression of envy in a destructive act. I shall have more to say of this implicit hatred of emotion and the need to avoid awareness of it.

In my fourth example—the report of the understanding girl and the haze—my understanding and his agreeable state of mind have been felt as a link between us which could give rise to a creative act. The link had been regarded with hate and transformed into a hostile and destructive sexuality rendering the patient–analyst couple sterile.

In my fifth example, of the two probability clouds, a capacity for understanding is the link which is being attacked, but the interest lies in the fact that the object making the destructive attacks is alien to the patient. Furthermore, the destroyer is making an attack on projective identification which is felt by the patient to be a method of communication. In so far as my supposed attack on his methods of communication is felt as possibly secondary to his envious attacks on me, he does not dissociate himself from feelings of guilt and responsibility. A further point is the appearance of judgement, which Freud regards as an essential feature of the dominance of the reality principle, among the ejected parts of the patient's personality. The fact that there were two probability clouds remained unexplained at the time, but in subsequent sessions I had material which led me to suppose that what had originally been an attempt to separate good from bad survived in the existence of two objects, but they were now similar in that each was a mixture of good and bad. Taking into consideration material from later sessions, I can draw conclusions which were not possible at the time; his capacity for judgement, which had been split up and destroyed with the rest of his ego and then ejected, was felt by him to be similar to other bizarre objects of the kind which I have described in my paper, 'Differentiation of the Psychotic from the Non-psychotic Personalities' [chapter 5]. These ejected particles were feared because of the treatment he had accorded them. He felt that the alienated judgement—the probability clouds—indicated that I was probably bad. His suspicion that the probability clouds were persecutory and hostile led him to doubt the value of the guidance they afforded him. They might supply him with a correct assessment or a deliberately false one, such as that a fact was an hallucination or vice versa; or would give rise to what, from a psychiatric point of view, we would call delusions. The probability clouds themselves had some qualities of a primitive breast and were felt to be enigmatic and intimidating.

In my sixth illustration, the report that a piece of iron had fallen on the floor, I had no occasion for interpreting an aspect of the material with which the patient had by this time become familiar. (I should perhaps say that experience had taught me that there were times when I assumed the patient's familiarity with some aspect of a situation with which we were dealing, only to discover that, in spite of the work that had been done upon it, he had forgotten it.) The familiar point that I did not interpret, but which is significant for the understanding of this episode, is that the patient's envy of the parental couple had been evaded by his substitution of himself and myself for the parents. The evasion failed, for the envy and hatred were now directed against him and me. The couple engaged in a creative act are felt to be sharing an enviable, emotional experience; he, being identified also with the excluded party, has a painful, emotional experience as well. On many occasions the patient, partly through experiences of the kind which I describe in this episode, and partly for reasons on which I shall enlarge later, had a hatred of emotion, and therefore, by a short extension, of life itself. This hatred contributes to the murderous attack on that which links the pair, on the pair itself, and on the object generated by the pair. In the episode I am describing, the patient is suffering the consequences of his early attacks on the state of mind that forms the link between the creative pair and his identification with both the hateful and creative states of mind.

In this, and the preceding illustration, there are elements that suggest the formation of a hostile persecutory object, or agglomeration of objects, which expresses its hostility in a manner of great importance in producing the predominance of psychotic mechanisms in a patient; the characteristics with which I have already invested the agglomeration of persecutory objects have the quality of a primitive, and even murderous, superego.

Curiosity, arrogance, and stupidity

95. In my paper 'On Arrogance' [chapter 7] I suggested that Freud's analogy of an archaeological investigation with a psychoanalysis is helpful if it is considered that we are exposing evidence not so much of a primitive civilization as of a primitive disaster. The value of the analogy is lessened because in the analysis we are confronted not so much with a static situation that permits leisurely study, but with a catastrophe that remains at one and the same moment actively vital and yet incapable of resolution into quiescence. This lack of progress in any direction must be attributed in part to the destruction of a capacity for curiosity and the consequent inability to learn, but before I go into this I must say something about a matter that plays hardly any part in the illustrations I have given.

Attacks on the link originate in what Melanie Klein (1948) calls the paranoid-schizoid phase. This period is dominated by part-object relationships. If it is borne in mind that the patient has a part-object relationship with himself as well as with objects not himself, it contributes to the understanding of phrases such as "it seems" which are commonly employed by the deeply disturbed patient on occasions when a less disturbed patient might say "I think" or "I believe". When he says "it seems" he is often referring to a feeling—an "it seems" feeling—which is a part of his psyche and yet is not observed as part of a whole object. The conception of the part-object as analogous to an anatomical structure, encouraged by the patient's employment of concrete images as units of thought, is misleading because the part-object relationship is not with the anatomical structures only but with function, not with anatomy but with physiology, not with the breast but with feeding, poisoning, loving, hating. This contributes to the impression of a disaster that is dynamic and not static. The problem that has to be solved on this early yet superficial level, must be stated in adult terms by the question, "What is something?"—not the question, "Why is something?", because "why" has, through guilt, been split off. Problems, the solution of which depends upon an awareness of causation, cannot therefore be stated, let alone solved. This produces a situation in which the patient appears to have no problems except those posed by the existence of analyst and patient. His preoccupation is with what is this or that function of which he is aware, though unable to grasp the totality of which the function is a part. It follows that there is never any question why the patient or the analyst is there, or why something is said or done or felt, nor can there be any question of attempting to alter the causes of some state of mind. Since "what?" can never be answered without "how?" or "why?", further difficulties arise. I shall leave this on one side to consider the mechanisms employed by the infant to solve the problem "what?", when it is felt in relation to a part-object relationship with a function.

Denial of normal degrees of projective identification

96. I employ the term 'link' because I wish to discuss the patient's relationship with a function rather than with the object that subserves a function; my concern is not only with the breast or penis or verbal thought, but with their function of providing the link between two objects.

In her 'Notes on Some Schizoid Mechanisms' (1946) Melanie Klein speaks of the importance of an excessive employment of splitting and projective identification in the production of a very disturbed personality. She also speaks of "the introjection of the good object, first of all the mother 's breast" as a "precondition for normal development". I shall suppose that there is a normal degree of projective identification, without defining the limits within which normality lies, and that associated with introjective identification this is the foundation on which normal development rests.

This impression derives partly from a feature in a patient's analysis which was difficult to interpret because it did not appear to be sufficiently obtrusive at any one moment for an interpretation to be supported by convincing evidence. Throughout the analysis the patient resorted to projective identification with a persistence suggesting it was a mechanism of which he had never been able sufficiently to avail himself; the analysis afforded him an opportunity for the exercise of a mechanism of which he had been cheated. I did not have to rely on this impression alone: there were sessions which led me to suppose that the patient felt there was some object that denied him the use of projective identification. In the illustrations I have given, particularly in the first (the stammer) and the fourth (the understanding girl and the blue haze) there are elements which indicate that the patient felt the parts of his personality that he wished to repose in me were refused entry by me, but there had been associations prior to this which led me to this view.

When the patient strove to rid himself of fears of death which were felt to be too powerful for his personality to contain, he split off his fears and put them into me, the idea apparently being that if they were allowed to repose there long enough they would undergo modification by my psyche and could then be safely reintrojected. On the occasion I have in mind the patient had felt, probably for reasons similar to those I give in my fifth illustration (the probability clouds), that I evacuated them so quickly that the feelings were not modified, but had become more painful.

Associations from a period in the analysis earlier than that from which these illustrations have been drawn, showed an increasing intensity of emotions in the patient. This originated in what he felt was my refusal to accept parts of his personality. Consequently he strove to force them into me with increased desperation and violence. His behaviour, isolated from the context of the analysis, might have appeared to be an expression of primary aggression: the more violent his phantasies of projective identification, the more frightened he became of me. There were sessions in which such behaviour expressed unprovoked aggression, but I quote this series because it shows the patient in a different light—his violence a reaction to what he felt was my hostile defensiveness. The analytic situation built up in my mind a sense of witnessing an extremely early scene. I felt that the patient had experienced in infancy a mother who dutifully responded to the infant's emotional displays. The dutiful response had in it an element of impatient, "I don't know what's the matter with the child." My deduction was that, in order to understand what the child wanted, the mother should have treated the infant's cry as more than a demand for her presence. From the infant's point of view she should have taken into her, and thus experienced, the fear that the child was dying. It was this fear that the child could not contain. He strove to split it off together with the part of the personality in which it lay and project it into the mother. An understanding mother is able to experience the feeling of dread, that this baby was striving to deal with by projective identification, and yet retain a balanced outlook. This patient had had to deal with a mother who could not tolerate experiencing such feelings and reacted either by denying them ingress, or alternatively by becoming a prey to the anxiety which resulted from introjection of the infant's feelings. The latter reaction must, I think, have been rare denial was dominant.

To some this reconstruction will appear to be unduly fanciful; to me it does not seem forced and is the reply to any who may object that too much stress is placed on the transference to the exclusion of a proper elucidation of early memories.

In the analysis a complex situation may be observed. The patient feels he is being allowed an opportunity of which he had hitherto been cheated; the poignancy of his deprivation is thereby rendered the more acute and so are the feelings of resentment at the deprivation. Gratitude for the opportunity coexists with hostility to the analyst as the person who will not understand and refuses the patient the use of the only method of communication by which he feels he can make himself understood. Thus the link between patient and analyst, or infant and breast, is the mechanism of projective identification. The destructive attacks upon this link originate in a source external to the patient or infant, namely the analyst or breast. The result is excessive projective identification by the patient and a deterioration of his developmental processes.

I do not put forward this experience as the cause of the patient's disturbance; that finds its main source in the inborn disposition of the infant as I described it in 'Differentiation of the Psychotic from the Non-psychotic Personalities' [chapter 5]. I regard it as a central feature of the environmental factor in the production of the psychotic personality.

Before I discuss this consequence for the patient's development, I must refer to the inborn characteristics and the part that they play in producing attacks by the infant on all that links him to the breast, namely, primary aggression and envy. The seriousness of these attacks is enhanced if the mother displays the kind of unreceptiveness which I have described, and is diminished, but not abolished, if the mother can introject the infant's feelings and remain balanced (Klein, 1957); the seriousness remains because the psychotic infant is overwhelmed with hatred and envy of the mother 's ability to retain a comfortable state of mind although experiencing the infant's feelings. This was clearly brought out by a patient who insisted that I must go through it with him, but was filled with hate when he felt I was able to do so without a breakdown. Here we have another aspect of destructive attacks upon the link, the link being the capacity of the analyst to introject the patient's projective identifications. Attacks on the link, therefore, are synonymous with attacks on the analyst's, and originally the mother 's, peace of mind. The capacity to introject is transformed by the patient's envy and hate into greed devouring the patient's psyche; similarly, peace of mind becomes hostile indifference. At this point analytic problems arise through the patient's employment (to destroy the peace of mind that is so much envied) of acting out, delinquent acts and threats of suicide.

Consequences

97. To review the main features so far: the origin of the disturbance is twofold. On the one hand there is the patient's inborn disposition to excessive destructiveness, hatred, and envy: on the other the environment which, at its worst, denies to the patient the use of the mechanisms of splitting and projective identification. On some occasions the destructive attacks on the link between patient and environment, or between different aspects of the patient's personality, have their origin in the patient; on others, in the mother, although in the latter instance and in psychotic patients, it can never be in the mother alone. The disturbances commence with life itself. The problem that confronts the patient is: What are the objects of which he is aware? These objects, whether internal or external, are in fact part-objects and predominantly, though not exclusively, what we should call functions and not morphological structures. This is obscured because the patient's thinking is conducted by means of concrete objects and therefore tends to produce, in the sophisticated mind of the analyst, an impression that the patient's concern is with the nature of the concrete object. The nature of the functions which excite the patient's curiosity he explores by projective identification. His own feelings, too powerful to be contained within his personality, are amongst these functions. Projective identification makes it possible for him to investigate his own feelings in a personality powerful enough to contain them. Denial of the use of this mechanism, either by the refusal of the mother to serve as a repository for the infant's feelings, or by the hatred and envy of the patient who cannot allow the mother to exercise this function, leads to a destruction of the link between infant and breast, and consequently to a severe disorder of the impulse to be curious on which all learning depends. The way is therefore prepared for a severe arrest of development. Furthermore, thanks to a denial of the main method open to the infant for dealing with his too powerful emotions, the conduct of emotional life, in any case a severe problem, becomes intolerable. Feelings of hatred are thereupon directed against all emotions including hate itself, and against external reality which stimulates them. It is a short step from hatred of the emotions to hatred of life itself. In 'Differentiation of the Psychotic from the Non-psychotic Personalities' I stated that this hatred results in a resort to projective identification of all the perceptual apparatus including the embryonic thought which forms a link between sense impressions and consciousness. The tendency to excessive projective identification when death instincts predominate is thus reinforced.

Superego

98. The early development of the superego is affected by this kind of mental functioning in a way I must now describe. As I have said, the link between infant and breast depends upon projective identification and a capacity to introject projective identifications. Failure to introject makes the external object appear intrinsically hostile to curiosity and to the method, namely projective identification, by which the infant seeks to satisfy it. Should the breast be felt as fundamentally understanding, it has been transformed by the infant's envy and hate into an object whose devouring greed has as its aim the introjection of the infant's projective identifications in order to destroy them. This can show in the patient's belief that the analyst strives, by understanding the patient, to drive him insane. The result is an object which, when installed in the patient, exercises the function of a severe and ego-destructive superego. This description is not accurate applied to any object in the paranoid-schizoid position because it supposes a whole-object. The threat that such a wholeobject impends contributes to the inability, described by Melanie Klein and others (Klein, 1946, 1948; Rosenfeld, 1952; Segal, 1950), of the psychotic patient to face the depressive position and the developments attendant on it. In the paranoid-schizoid phase the bizarre objects composed partially of elements of a persecutory super-ego which I described in 'Differentiation of the Psychotic from the Nonpsychotic Personalities' are predominant.

Arrested development

The disturbance of the impulse of curiosity on which all learning depends, and the denial of the mechanism by which it seeks expression, makes normal development impossible. Another feature obtrudes if the course of the analysis is favourable; problems which in sophisticated language are posed by the question "Why?" cannot be formulated. The patient appears to have no appreciation of causation and will complain of painful states of mind while persisting in courses of action calculated to produce them. Therefore when the appropriate material presents itself the patient must be shown that he has no interest in why he feels as he does. Elucidation of the limited scope of his curiosity issues in the development of a wider range and an incipient preoccupation with causes. This leads to some modification of conduct which otherwise prolongs his distress.

Conclusions

99. The main conclusions of this paper relate to that state of mind in which the patient's psyche contains an internal object which is opposed to, and destructive of, all links whatsoever from the most primitive (which I have suggested is a normal degree of projective identification) to the most sophisticated forms of verbal communication and the arts.

In this state of mind emotion is hated; it is felt to be too powerful to be contained by the immature psyche, it is felt to link objects and it gives reality to objects which are not self and therefore inimical to primary narcissism.

The internal object which in its origin was an external breast that refused to introject, harbour, and so modify the baneful force of emotion, is felt, paradoxically, to intensify, relative to the strength of the ego, the emotions against which it initiates the attacks. These attacks on the linking function of emotion lead to an over-prominence in the psychotic part of the personality of links which appear to be logical, almost mathematical, but never emotionally reasonable. Consequently the links surviving are perverse, cruel, and sterile.

The external object which is internalized, its nature, and the effect when so established on the methods of communication within the psyche and with the environment, are left for further elaboration later.

Commentary on "Attacks on linking"

W. R. Bion

In **91**, the reference to the destruction of an important link is based on a number of observations, the cumulative effect of which led to the formulations in the paper, 'Attacks on Linking'. The ideas set out in it illuminate a number of situations which I did not have in mind when I wrote the paper. As I became able to observe the evolution of the psychoanalytic situation I was led to the frustrating aspects of memory and desire. Analysands stimulate both elements in the analyst as a method of destroying his link with the analysand. It is as if the patient were himself a psychoanalyst who discovered these elements and set about deliberately to stimulate them to destroy the link between the analyst and himself. Experience of attempting to exclude the operation of memory and desire has persuaded me of the value of doing so. The difficulty of successful exclusion makes it hard to define memory and desire with rigour, or to assess the nature of the sharpening of intuition associated with it. I regard the idea of causation, implicit throughout the paper, as erroneous; it will limit the perspicacity of the analyst if he allows this element in 'Attacks on Linking' to obtrude. The 'causal link' has apparent validity only with events associated closely in space and time. The fallacious nature of reasoning based on the idea of 'causes' is clearly argued by

Heisenberg,[1] in terms which should evoke an understanding response in any psychoanalyst. Provided the analyst does not allow himself to be beguiled into searching for and proposing 'causes', except in conversational terms, the paper may stimulate enquiries of his own. The discovery of a 'cause' relates more to the peace of mind of the discoverer than to the object of his research.

This brings me to the problem of how the gap is to be bridged between reading the papers in this book and the psychoanalytic experience. My suggestion is that the papers should be read in the same conditions as those in which a psychoanalysis should be conducted—without memory or desire. And then forgotten. They can be re-read; but not remembered. Such advice could be given with greater assurance if the nature of the communications, their status as formulations, were more certain. I have attempted to make that so by proposing that so-called clinical reports (supposedly F3) were regarded as C3-verbal transformations of sensory impressions. At this early stage, there is no adequate categorization which is likely to be more useful than popular repute.

The proper state for intuiting psychoanalytic realizations, which I have suggested in this review, can be compared with the states supposed to provide conditions for hallucinations. The hallucinated individual is apparently having sensuous experiences without any background of sensuous reality. The analyst must be able to intuit psychic reality which has no known sensuous realization. The hallucinated individual transforms and interprets the background of reality, of which he is aware, in different terms from those employed by the psychoanalyst. I do not consider that the hallucinated patient is reporting a realization with a sensuous background; equally I do not consider an interpretation in psychoanalysis derives from facts accessible to sensuous apparatus. How then is one to explain the difference between an hallucination and an interpretation of an intuited psychoanalytic experience? The charge is sometimes loosely and lightly made that psychoanalysts analysing patients who are psychotic are themselves psychotic. I would seek a formulation to represent the difference between the intuition (in my sense of the term) of a realization, which has no sensible component, and a hallucination of a realization which is similarly devoid of a sensible realization. The

[1] *Physics and Philosophy* (Allen & Unwin, 1958), p. 81.

psychoanalyst has at least the opportunity which would allow him to contribute an answer; many supposedly sane and responsible people transform thoughts into actions which it would be charitable to call insane and are often, charitably, so called.

As a stimulus to further thought, I would draw attention to a peculiarity, known to all but not sufficiently regarded. Ordinarily the sense organs have their own objects of sense. It is true that the eye, subjected to pressure, will apparently 'see' light ('stars', according to pugilists). In the mental realm, the "sense organ of psychic reality" (to borrow a phrase from Freud) has no such limitation. It can indifferently appreciate all the counterparts of *all* the senses. The mental counterparts of smell, sight, etc., can *all* apparently be intuited by the same apparatus. The issue is of practical importance to the analyst whose analysand says, "I see what you mean" when he has an hallucination, say, of being sexually assaulted; what *he* means is that the *meaning* of what the analyst said appeared to him in a visual form and *not* that he understood an interpretation. This is the kind of problem to which the last paper, 'A Theory of Thinking' [chapter 9], is an introduction.

The fact that thinking and talking play such an important part in psychoanalysis is so obvious that it is liable to escape attention. It does not, however, escape the attention of the patient who is concentrating his attacks on linking, and in particular the link between himself and the analyst; such a patient makes destructive attacks on the capacity of both analyst and himself to talk or think. If these attacks are to be properly understood, the analyst needs to be aware of the nature of the targets being attacked. The paper is an attempt to elucidate this. With my present experience I would lay more stress, in **98**, on the importance of doubting that a thinker is necessary because thoughts exist. For a proper understanding of the situation when attacks on linking are being delivered, it is useful to postulate thoughts that have no thinker. I cannot here discuss the problems, but need to formulate them for further investigation, thus:—Thoughts exist without a thinker. The idea of infinitude is prior to any idea of the finite. The finite is "won from the dark and formless infinite". Restating this more concretely, the human personality is aware of infinity, the 'oceanic feeling'. It becomes aware of limitation, presumably through physical and mental experience of itself and the sense of frustration. A number that is infinite, a sense of infinity, is replaced, say, by a sense of threeness. The sense that an infinite number of objects exists is replaced by a sense that only three objects exist; infinite space becomes finite space. The thoughts which have no thinker acquire, or are acquired by, a thinker.

In practice I have found this formulation, or something like it, a helpful approximation to psychoanalytic realizations. The patient who suffers from what used to be known as 'disturbances of thought' will provide instances showing that every interpretation the analyst gives is really a thought of his. He will betray his belief that papers or books written by others, including of course his analyst, were really filched from him. This belief extends to what in more usual patients appears as the Oedipal situation. In so far as he or she admits the facts of parental intercourse, or verbal intercourse between the analyst and himself, he is simply a lump of faeces, the product of a couple. In so far as he regards himself as his creator, he has evolved out of the infinite. His human qualities (limitations) are due to the parents, by their intercourse, stealing him from himself (equated with God). The ramifications of this attitude, more clearly discerned if the analyst postulates "thoughts without a thinker", are so considerable that I require another book to attempt elucidation. Inadequate though this formulation is, I hope it will help the reader to find the continuation of the developments which I have tried to sketch out in these papers.

"Attacks on Linking" Revisited

CHAPTER ONE

Disconnection: a new look at narcissism

Ronald Britton

Bion's development of his concept of "attacks on linking" was part of his exploration of the "psychotic personality" and the part it played in psychotic and non-psychotic neurotic disorders (Bion, 1967a[1957], 1967b[1959]) He considered that a "psychotic personality" co-existed with a "non-psychotic personality" in psychotic disorders and in severe neuroses, with the psychotic personality dominant in the former and masked by a more dominant neurotic pathological organisation in the latter. He also suggested that in the psychotic personality, projective identification substituted for regression in the neurotic personality. The projective identification he refers to in this passage is of an extreme order in which the ego's experience of reality is fragmented and projected, sometimes into inanimate objects. Thus, the elements provided by Freud's reality principle, "that is to say, consciousness of sense impressions, attention, memory, judgment, thought" (Bion, 1967b[1959], p. 47) are lost through projection.

At the heart of this "psychotic personality" was "an omnipotent phantasy that is intended to destroy either reality or the awareness of it, and thus to achieve a state that is neither life nor death" (Bion, 1967b[1959], p. 46). In other words, that if the mental representation of something could be eliminated, this would eliminate the actual "something". In this supposed state of affairs, the eradication of awareness of an object by elimination of its psychic representation would mean that the actual link, the sensory connection to an object, would be wiped out. An example from the history of psychoanalysis, the case of Anna O as described by Breuer, can illustrate it. She had negative hallucinations: that is, in one phase of her disorder, she was completely perceptually unaware of the physical presence of anyone other than Breuer (Freud, 1895d). This was part of a severe case of what was rightly described as hysteria; the use of a psychotic mechanism in this neurosis is complementary to Bion's theory and perhaps illustrates the usefulness of the "old-fashioned" psychiatric term, hysterical psychosis. Anna O omnipotently created a subjective, perceptual world that included only herself and her doctor.

In the cases Bion wished to characterise as manifesting features of the "psychotic personality", the connections with anything outside the "self" were completely eliminated. Within my own psychiatric experience, the clinical picture most resembling this was in some cases of catatonic schizophrenia in the days before antipsychotic medication became commonplace. In this state, which could be regarded as resembling a theoretical state of primary narcissism, there is imputably only a central self with no relationships other than to itself. But if one posits, as Melanie Klein did, that an object relation exists from the outset of any self-awareness, this self–self relationship is originally a self–object relationship. In "attacks on linking" the omnipotent phantasy has changed subject–object into subject–subject: fusion instead of connection. We could describe this in terms of projective identification.

If we take the first object relationship to be container–contained, that is, self inside something or something inside self, once this has been replaced by self–self, it is then a self contained by itself or a self containing itself. If, as I believe, we experience the mind/self as in the body or the body as in the mind/self, an alternation that is the normal experience of body–mind relations, then, by phantasied disconnection, the mind is only inside itself and the body is only an idea of the mind. The outside world is only an extension of the self; there is no outer world or, indeed, any other world.

I have never had the opportunity of analysing a schizophrenic patient in a catatonia, which one can think of as the ultimate disconnected state of mind. The psychotic patients one does meet clinically in analysis are more partial in this respect and one relies on contact with the non-psychotic personality of the patient, which, as Bion said, is always a latent or hidden presence in psychotic illnesses. My own experience with a chronic psychotic patient, in an analysis that lasted twenty years, is that this is so. In her case, her mind was dominated by thoughts from her psychotic personality and, in effect, they terrorised her non-psychotic self. Her quasi-neurotic solution was to produce a pathological organisation that aimed to rid herself of all her thoughts since she took all thought as arising from her psychotic personality. Her methods were to attempt to eradicate her thoughts by physical symbolic evacuations such as flushing the toilet repeatedly, closing doors behind herself innumerable times in the hope of leaving her mind in the room she had just left, and so on. This was a defensive use of projective identification that, alas, created an even more dangerous external world for her that was full of her evacuated thoughts. She managed to place this world outside the small portion of London she and I both inhabited, which meant she could live within it but not travel anywhere beyond it. She was undiagnosable, according to psychiatrists who, taking her symptomatology to be obsessive–compulsive, tried to locate her as such but were unable to accommodate her multiple delusions within the diagnosis. Once in analysis, the chronic psychosis was evident and the defensive rituals could be seen for what they were.

However, our lack of access to the ideas of the manifest psychotic personality, such as that described by Bion, can be compensated by considering the works of artists committed to a similar system as an ideology. One such was William Blake in the early eighteenth century, and another was Kazmir Malevich in the twentieth century. The latter wrote of his new movement,

> Suprematism is the beginning of a new culture. Our world of art has become new, non-objective, and pure. Everything has disappeared; a mass of material is left from which a new form will be built . . . The artist can be a creator only when the forms in his picture have nothing in common with nature. (Malevich, 1915)

The iconic picture of this movement was his *Black Square* (1915), which eliminated all forms in the picture that the visiting eye expected to see.

Similarly, Blake wrote, "I must invent a system or be enslaved to another man's". He regarded his imagination as the divine source, the creator, and he regarded belief as the act of creation; self-doubt he saw as destruction.

> If the Sun and Moon should Doubt
> They'd immediately Go out.
>
> (Keynes, 1959, p. 433)

He saw belief as truth; formed by imagination and not received by perception; not seeing is believing but believing is seeing. He wrote that, ". . . vision is the world of imagination: is Eternity. Vision is all that exists", and he claimed, "Mental things alone are real". The eye is an organ for projection not perception:

> This Life's dim Windows of the Soul
> Distorts the Heavens from Pole to Pole
> And leads you to Believe a Lie
> When you see with, not thro' the Eye
>
> (Keynes, 1959, p. 753)

Belief, treated as fact, was, for him, the limiting membrane of an otherwise bottomless void, the only curb on the total mental disintegration that followed the act of creation. Creation, he thought, resulted in the catastrophic separating out of the intellect from within the primal unity of the self. The intellect he saw as attached to the illusion of a finite, measurable, physical world. He had two versions of this catastrophe. In the first, Urizen (a pun on your reason), who is the personification of intellect, creates a fathomless void in the personality by detaching himself from the whole body of the eternal self by his attachment to the world of physical sensation. In the second account of catastrophic creation, Los, imagination personified, is confronted with an impenetrable, material, objective world created by Urizen, a solid non-fluctuant object. Los was driven wild with impatience by this black, adamantine, impenetrable, reality rock created by Urizen. So he smashed it to pieces, thus producing a bottomless abyss into which he then fell.

So, we have in the first version the subjective account of a prenatal quiescent psychic unity ruptured by a part of mental life that, by linking itself to the physical senses, tears itself off, leaving a chasm within the self. In the second account, the infant imagination, in its frustration and antipathy to reality represented as an impenetrable, black, cold object of adamantine hardness, smashes it to fragments and then falls into the abyss thus created.

> . . . Los fell & fell
> Sunk precipitant, heavy, down, down,
> Times on times, night on night, day on day.
> Truth has bounds error none; falling, falling;
> Years on Years, ages on ages,
> Still he fell thro' the void, still a void
>
> (Keynes, 1959, p. 258)

This second version of Blake's strongly resembles that described by Melanie Klein as the destructive attack on the internal object resulting in states of mental fragmentation. "The mechanism of one part of the ego annihilating other parts . . . I suggest underlies *world catastrophe*", she wrote (Klein, 1946, p. 24). Bion, in several of his writings, emphasised this notion of Klein that the patient attacks his object with such violence that not only is the object felt to disintegrate, but also the mental apparatus of the person delivering the attack. This poetic account by Blake describes this and the ensuing symptomatology in an extraordinarily vivid way.

The mind then falls into the abyss of unknowingness thus created. As it falls, it labours to produce a belief system that it can treat as the truth, the "bounds" it needs to arrest its fall. Earlier, Blake had propounded a dictum of absolutist subjectivity so that "Everything possible to be believed is an image of truth" (Keynes, 1959, p. 151); so, the belief system the mind creates "as an image of the truth" serves as its own safety net and remedy for chaos and the void. The enemies of this belief are, therefore, the enemies of self-existence and the creators of chaos. The sceptics, *the Questioners*, as Blake calls them, are, therefore, the enemies of the mind. Professional questioners such as empirical or natural philosophers are the agents of Satan: Bacon, Locke, and Newton in particular: Bacon for seeking truth through reason as opposed to revelation; Locke for his emphasis on learning through experience as opposed to Blake's belief that "Man is a garden ready planted and sown" (Johnson & Grant, 1979, p. 443); Newton for formulating the laws of nature in a material universe that Blake abhorred and proof by mathematics which he despised. "*Science* is the Tree of Death", wrote Blake (Keynes, 1959, p. 777). The only safety net and remedy for world catastrophe is psychotic delusion.

We, as analysts, would do well to bear in mind the way Blake sees the realistic or reasoning doubters as the dangerous agents of chaos. Analysis, with its inbuilt scepticism, can be seen to be dangerous to patients with such beliefs and they will try to avoid analysis even while in it. They might well be attached to the analyst in a positive transference while treating analysis as potentially catastrophic.

Blake, interestingly, offers us alternative reasons for disconnection from the internal representation of the psychical world and these one could see similarly as psychoanalytic alternatives. In one, the primal unity, we might call it "primary narcissism", is ruptured by an attachment in the first object relationship. There is now a gap in the inner world. In other words, an object relationship divides the self. In the second, the primacy of the infinitely, immediately satisfying pleasure principle is challenged by the adamantine nature of reality with its finite space and measurable time. This arouses such fury that its internal connections are smashed. Frustration, or, rather, intolerance of frustration, is the provocation and destruction is its outcome. Is the individual's disconnection from the outside world and its internal representatives regression or destruction? Freud appeared to think of regression while Abraham saw it as intolerance of object love and implied aggression. This difference of opinion persists in psychoanalytic theorising, resurfacing in different views of narcissistic disorders as defensive and libidinal or destructive.

This difference, I think, disappears if, instead of thinking of narcissism as primary and object love as secondary, they could be seen as coincident and conflicting from the beginning. But I would propose that they are not both positive drives or impulses, that it is not narcissism *vs.* socialism, as Bion puts it. Narcissism can be seen not as a force in its own right, but as a negative reaction to connection to objects because they are not identical and, thus, arouse a psychic immune response of hostility. It could be said to be not auto-erotism but auto-immunity. It applies physio-pathologically when part of the body is wrongly identified as alien and is attacked by the immune system. So it could be with mental parts of the self, which are attacked by the mental immune system. It is as if a social body, such as a nation or a religion, decides that part of its population was foreign and decided to annihilate it.

Anyway, in whatever way it arises, connection is the provocation and the psychotic solution is disconnection. This drastic solution means psychotic illness in which survival is dependent on unacknowledged others or some sort of compromise that evades complete disconnection while avoiding the catastrophic object relationship. A pathological organisation producing a neurosis or personality disorder is one such compromise. I shall describe one particular example where self and object are psychically interchangeable as if they were two halves of one object.

This alternating system, which I have described elsewhere as the basis of as-if personality (Britton, 1998), is only possible in a dyadic relationship. If the object has a visible relationship independently of the self, the subject–object identity is fractured. This can be avoided by splitting the ego in the way Freud described as disavowal. In this case, the subject–object relationship was maintained by severing the psychic connections between the two parental figures.

I would like to begin my discussion of just such a defensive organisation from the analysis of a patient, Mr B, whom I shall discuss. His dreams showed his fear of projection because of the terrifying, inescapable, external world he would create if he amalgamated his inner objects with external objects. His fear of introjection was as great because of the substantive reality it would give to his phantasied internal, savagely consuming objects.

He lived psychically, therefore neither internally nor externally, but in no-man's-land. His aim in analysis was to find agreement, not to adopt my ideas or to impose his own. His technique was either to find a way to stimulate an interpretation corresponding to his already existing idea, or to tread water with vague, verbose material until I made an interpretation which he could then illustrate with his associations. We were like the pantomime horse, two men in one skin. He had dream images that illustrated the relationship: for example, two men in one shirt, each with one arm in each sleeve. In another dream, he and his mother were driving a car, each with a hand on either side of the steering wheel. Alternating with this was another car that had the same arrangement but in this it was with his father.

When he first came to analysis, he had virtually no childhood memories but made a few fixed statements about the past that were invariant; his accounts of them were always couched in the same phrases. One such statement was that his parents lived in the same house, but on different floors, throughout his childhood. Subsequently, it became clear that the reality of their relationship gave some substance to this account but that it was a caricature. It served to structure his phantasy that he was involved with each parent separately. In all his phantasies, the positive and negative versions of the Oedipus complex were treated as reversible, inverse parallels which would never converge. This appeared to form a prototype for the organisation of his internal object world. They existed like alternative universes in which all qualities and directions were simply reversed. The two parents were like two opposite magnetic poles that alternately orientated him. Thus, ambivalence was evaded while these alternatives existed and convergence was replaced by negative symmetry.

A dream will illustrate what I mean. In the dream, Mr B had gone to see his male dentist, where he met an attractive woman receptionist with whom he developed a relationship instead of seeing the dentist. His associations to the dream made it clear that the woman represented my wife. The scene changed in the dream and he found himself on the analytic couch lying between the woman and myself on the couch. The arrangement was such that the woman's head was at the end of the couch where my feet were, so that Mr B had to change from one end of the couch to the other in order to lie beside either. He was continually oscillating from one position to the other between the two figures in the course of the dream and there was something sexual about this movement.

I would suggest that it represented the insertion of Mr B into the primal scene so that he took over the sexual movement of the parents by his oscillating movement between them and dismantled the primal scene into his two inverse relationships. These then formed the basis for the "cleavage of his ego"—two diametrically opposed identifications. By this means, he formed a half identity in projective identification with one object and another with its negative. This arrangement, while giving expression to a fundamental antipathy to objects, also enabled him to secure object attachment while maintaining internal coherence. This was, I think, the basis of his defensive or pathological organisation in which he hoped to evade the natural convergence of the depressive position.

Other crucial distinctions that are, in reality, *asymmetrical* are treated as if they were *symmetrical* inversions. True/false; love/hate; child/adult; psychic/material are all antitheses which are not symmetrical but asymmetrical. In this, they are unlike up/down; left/

right; front/back; clockwise/anticlockwise, which are symmetrical inversions.

He dreamt of reversible situations and of objects that could turn themselves inside out so that their "inside skin" became their "outside skin". Such was the structure of his psychic organisation that these two worlds were simply antitheses of each other, like two sides of a mirror. His perceptions were often treated as reversibly interchangeable with ideas, which contradicted them as if they had the same claim on his belief. In his dreams, top might become bottom; right become left; north become south; bass become treble; white notes become black notes; back become front.

Mr B had what Freud might have called a neurotic character disorder and what I would term, following John Steiner (Steiner, 1987), a pathological organisation. This enabled him to disconnect from object relationships in conformity with his psychotic personality while retaining a neurotic relationship to reality.

Through the use of projective identification, he produced half subjective–half objective relationships that enabled him to constantly change places with his object. It was, in other words, a narcissistic object relationship. He was like a semi-detached house that shared an outside wall with its neighbour but had separate front doors.

This reversible perspective is necessarily dyadic; it cannot be maintained if a third object enters the scene. The self–object interchangeability is lost when the object has a link to another object and triangularity is introduced. The method used by my patient always resulted in parallel lines and never triangles until a later stage in analysis when he confronted the Oedipus situation as if for the first time as a triangular arrangement rather than two alternative parallel relationships.

Discussion

I would like to discuss Bion's concept of the psychotic personality characterised by severance of its connection with the perceptual world with the familiar psychoanalytic concept of narcissism as a force or predisposition in the personality that opposes object relations.

This notion of disconnection in psychosis, that is, in dementia praecox (schizophrenia), was first put forward by Abraham in 1907: he wrote to Freud, "I believe what in cases of chronic mental illness is called dementia is nothing but the patient shutting himself away from the world, the withdrawal of libido from persons and objects" (Abraham & Freud, 1965, p. 6). He added, "The insufficient development of object-love appears to be an inhibition in the maturation of the personality" (Abraham & Freud, 1965, p. 7). Freud readily agreed with this, as can be seen in their correspondence; their first letters were written before Abraham actually met Freud (Abraham & Freud, 1965). Freud saw this withdrawal of libido as regression to auto-erotism in individuals who had inadequately completed the necessary development from auto-erotism to object-love. Abraham's account, though it does not contradict Freud, sounds more like an active repudiation of object relations and, in this respect, it is more like the subsequent, much later, version that Bion based on Melanie Klein's work and adopted in "Attacks on linking". The wording of his title implies an aggressive motive, which is why I prefer the less committed term "disconnection", as it leaves open the aetiology and possible reasons for the severance.

If we adopt Klein's model of infancy in which introjection is the beginning of extra-uterine life, then we can see disconnection as preventing it. Klein wrote of introjection as

> in his phantasy he takes into himself every thing which he perceives in the outside world . . . Not only the mouth . . . for instance, the child breathes in, takes in through his eyes, his ears, through touch and so on. (Klein, 1936, p. 291).

By disconnection there is no introjection; it is cancelled by disconnection, or, to be more precise, if introjection is a phantasy, a counter-phantasy can eliminate it. Disconnection is a process that, in phantasy, annihilates all phantasies based on introjection. This would then resemble what has been described as "primary narcissism", which, in earlier psychoanalysis, was thought of as a pre-object-related developmental phase. I am suggesting, in line with Klein and Bion, that it is an aspiration, not a developmental stage, that total disconnection from the world of external perception and internal sensation is due to an effort to be rid of object relatedness. In the world of the arts, I have talked of Blake's claim that imagination and not perception should create the world. Also, in the past century, Malevich strove to free painting from nature and to substitute abstract forms. His black square was composed by the elimination of anything but black: "The artist can be a creator only when forms in his picture have nothing in common with nature", and his "white forms against a white background" represented "a final liberation from the world of visible forms" (Malevich, 1915). Even hallucination might be rendered invisible, such is the urge to eliminate perception of natural forms. A psychotic patient of Bion had what Bion calls "invisible hallucinations", "He sat up", said Bion, "and stared intently into space. I said he seemed to be seeing something. He reported that he could not see what he saw" (Bion, 1967b[1959], p. 95).

I would like to suggest, however, that "narcissism", in the sense of the abolition of object relations, is not primary but is reactive. That it is a psychic immune response to the ingestion (introjection) of objects that are not identical with the self. In its most extreme form, which Bion characterises as the psychotic personality, it also annihilates those aspects and functions of the ego.

As Klein said, if one part of the ego annihilates another, that produces what is phantasied to be the "world catastrophe" (Klein, 1946, p. 109). The non-psychotic personality, therefore, regards the psychotic personality as its greatest threat and the defensive organisations it produces in an attempt to safeguard itself are manifest as neuroses and neurotic characteristics. These include what are often described as narcissistic disorders and it is as well for analysts to keep in mind the defensive function of these pathological organisations, which the patient regards as necessary to prevent domination by the psychotic personality. This means that some patients believe that their pathological organisation is keeping madness at bay, and analysis, therefore, is felt to be a potential threat and the analyst a mad enthusiast. One such patient of mine, with a narcissistic disorder and a history of an adolescent psychotic breakdown, dreamt, when under way in his analysis, of driving a car along a cliff and a traffic policeman confidently waving him onwards over the cliff edge. In such circumstances, the positive transference can attach the patient to the person of the analyst but not to the analysis. In such cases, the patient's fear that free association and acknowledgement of transference love would lead to madness needs to be exposed repeatedly. Only after this has been worked through does a freer relationship develop between the patient and his/her hidden thoughts.

In this chapter, I have emphasised the underlying or manifest psychotic urge to disconnect arising from psychic allergy to foreign objects and the perceptions they give rise to. This is not the only source of opposition to introjection that might manifest itself during analysis; there is an alternative which one could describe as traumatic. In this sense, it is similar to the differentiation I made between destructive and libidinal narcissism, following Rosenfeld (Britton, 2008). This traumatic object-phobia arises, I believe, where the fear is of intrusive projective identification by the object, probably with a history of such projection in the infantile primary relationship and subsequent analogous experiences in the oedipal situation. This scenario needs to be distinguished from the attacks on links described by Bion, referred to in this chapter as disconnection.

It is not too difficult to do this in analysis, but it is difficult to describe, as it is largely a matter of countertransference affect. Roughly speaking, I would say the first situation is found in narcissistic and psychotic disorders, while the latter is found in hysteria; each has its own characteristic countertransference. In this respect, it returns us to the very first discussion of these differences by Abraham,

> In the one case the libido is withdrawn from objects, in the other it cathects objects in an excessive degree. On the one hand there is a loss of the capacity of sublimation, and on the other increased capacity for it. (Abraham, 1973[1908], p. 77)

The theoretical understanding of these states has been enlarged and changed, and I am suggesting a further addition with the notion of psychic atopia, but the phenomenology remains the same. This, I think, is a testimony to clinical psychoanalysis and the discoveries it makes.

References

Abraham, H., & Freud, E. (Eds.) (1965). *A Psycho-Analytic Dialogue: The Letters of Sigmund Freud and Karl Abraham*. London: Hogarth.

Abraham, K. (1973)[1908]. The psycho-sexual differences between hysteria and dementia praecox. In: *The Selected Papers of Karl Abraham* (pp. 64–79). London: Hogarth.

Bion, W. R. (1967a)[1957]. Differentiation of the psychotic from the non-psychotic personalities. In: *Second Thoughts* (pp. 43–64). New York: Jason Aronson.

Bion, W. R. (1967b)[1959]. Attacks on linking. In: *Second Thoughts* (pp. 93–109). New York: Jason Aronson.

Britton, R. (1998). The suspension of belief. In: *Belief and Imagination* (pp. 59–68). London: Routledge.

Britton, R. (2008). What part does narcissism play in narcissistic disorders? In: J. Steiner (Ed.), *Rosenfeld in Retrospect* (pp. 22–34). London: Routledge.

Freud, S. [with Breuer, J.] (1895d). *Studies on Hysteria*. *S. E., 2*. London: Hogarth.

Johnson, M. L., & Grant, J. E. (1979). *Blake's Poetry and Designs*. New York: Norton.

Keynes, G. (Ed.) (1959). *Blake: Complete Writings*. Oxford: Oxford University Press.

Klein, M. (1936). Weaning. In: R. E. Money-Kyrle (Ed.), *The Writings of Melanie Klein, Volume I* (pp. 290–305). London: Hogarth Press, 1975.

Klein, M. (1946). Notes on some schizoid mechanisms. *International Journal of Psychoanalysis, 27*: 99–110.

Malevich, K. (1915). Suprematist, The Artchive. Malevich Black Square, Tate Gallery.

Steiner, J. (1987). The interplay between pathological organisations and the paranoid–schizoid and depressive positions. *International Journal of Psychoanalysis, 68*: 69–80.

CHAPTER TWO

"Attacks on linking" revisited: clinical material revisited twenty years later

Clara Nemas

To revisit a concept means to look at it from the perspective of a double arrow between the present and the past. In a retrospective look, we might find that a certain concept has not only endured the test of time but has become a powerful tool for understanding problems for which it was not designed in the first place. Links and their counterpart as hostility towards linking functions proposed by Bion in 1959 is one of these concepts which have had such a fertile effect in contemporary psychoanalysis.

The idea of the link, the linking function that connects human beings, and its vicissitudes is one of Bion's major contributions to our way of thinking, understanding, and working with our patients and with ourselves. At the same time, it poses problems that are difficult to solve in the analytic setting not very different from the ones created by the introduction of the concept of envy by Melanie Klein, from which it develops and also differs.

Klein and Bion have dwelled on the sources of unbearable pain in the internal world of patients, thus nurturing our understanding of the conflicts that are displayed in the transference.

Some brief reflections on Klein's objects relations and Bion's links

Kleinian theory, with its emphasis on unconscious object relations, is a theory of presences in which the most primitive experiences are responsible for deeply unconscious phantasies that are represented by objects or part-object relationships. For Klein, object relations exist from the beginning, the first object being the mother's breast and the mother, and the whole of her theory is a description of how and why these object relations are embedded in a world of phantasies at work from the earliest moments of life.

The fact that we are so dependent on our objects and, at the same time, we are so alone awakes all types of struggle in our relations throughout life. As infants, we have to deal with our own aggression and anger at our frailty and dependency. The baby wants to have the breast, and the failure to do so, which, essentially, implies recognition of the separate existence of the mother, can provoke feelings of rage, frustration, and violence that might actually spoil the good feeding experience when the breast becomes available. The complexity of the interaction between love and hostility, present from the beginning, opens up the field for recognition of the damage done to the loved object and the urge towards reparation.

In 1957, Klein wrote,

> Throughout my work I have attributed fundamental importance to the infant's first object relation – the relation to the breast and to the mother – and have drawn the conclusion that if this primal object, which is introjected, takes root in the ego with relative security, the basis for a satisfactory development is laid. (Klein, 1975[1957], p. 178)

The work demanded of the human infant is to face a reality that has to be accepted: that of our separateness, our dependence on objects we do not control, and of our relation to parents whose independent intercourse has to be acknowledged. Projective identification, with all its nuances and complexities, has, at its base, the intention to blur the painful separation between self and object.

Very early in his work on psychosis, Bion extended the Kleinian concept of projective identification to include its function as a means of communication between baby and mother. He stressed the importance of the linking function between minds as the basis for human development and considered that an emotional experience cannot be conceived of in isolation from a relationship.

> I employ the term "link" because I wish to discuss the patient's relationship with a function rather than with the object that subserves a function; my concern is not only with the breast, or penis, or verbal thought, but with their function of providing the link between the two objects. (Bion, 1967[1959], p. 102)

In this realm, reverie is a mysterious—not always present—emotional state that underlines and illuminates object relations and the birth of the psyche from the beginning of life. This function describes, in the best of cases, a natural capacity in the mind of the mother that allows her to accept, to lodge, and transform the baby's primitive non-verbal communication into alpha elements capable of thinking thoughts and feeling feelings. The most important outcome is the introjection by the baby of this maternal capacity—not the introjection of the breast as the prototype of the primal object. This introjected maternal capacity promotes the incipient capacity of the baby to tolerate his own psychic qualities; in other words, it allows us to be able to own our emotional states without (much) denial or projection.

Bion's proposal has helped us to understand that thinking is making links and that these links (K—knowledge is his more original contribution to the understanding of links) are emotional in origin and start preverbally as concrete perceptions of our relation to others in the internal and external worlds. Attacks on linking functions are attacks on thinking about the meaning of our relatedness.

When Hanna Arendt wrote about Eichmann's trial in Jerusalem, his lack of humanity struck her as a lack of capacity for thought. The recognition of our capacity for thinking and tolerating separateness and difference has to be acknowledged as well as an unconscious world that can attack the most basic emotional links that make understanding possible (Steuerman, 2000).

Attacks on linking and its roots in envy

It is not possible, I think, to approach and revisit Bion's concept of attacks on linking without reference to Klein's concept of envy, from which the former derives.

Envy, for Klein, is a basic emotion, common to all human beings, starting from the beginning of life. For her, the primary nature of envy has to do with the first object—the breast—as well as with its singularity of being endogenous, that is, that it positions itself beyond any frustration.

Envy is an everyday emotion, known to everyone and there are, throughout literature and religion, abundant references to, and descriptions of, envy and its workings. But it was not until "Envy and gratitude" (1975[1957]) (although there are earlier references to it) that we could consider envy not only as part of the empirical data, but also as a theoretical term belonging to a conceptual frame: an economic hypothesis that links an emotion with the death instinct. Within the Kleinian conceptualisation of mental life, envy is an impulse that generates a pathological splitting that impairs the introjection of a good object as the central core of the ego.

"Attacks on linking" is a conceptual tool that can only be understood within the frame of Bion's theory of thinking. It is derived from his work with psychotic patients, in whom he was able to uncover the intimate ways in which a part of the personality damages the very functions that make thought possible.

The main difference between the concept of envy and of attacks on linking resides in the direction of hostility. Bion describes a complex situation in which envy and envious attacks are launched not against an object—the good breast—but at the creative link, the couple engaged in a creative act. The links are the bridges that connect objects; objects are the pillars on which the bridge is sustained. ". . . the destructive attacks which the patient makes on anything which is felt to have the function of linking one object with another" (Bion, 1967[1959] p. 93).These ideas, of course, have deep roots in Kleinian developments on object relations but, at the same time, have an originality that marks a new way of thinking about human bonds in which thinking and verbal thought are basic.

However, there is still another complication to be faced. From "Envy and gratitude" (1975[1957]), there has been a change in the paradigm regarding the centrality of the presence of the object. The main problem to be faced by the infant has to do with the frustration provoked not by the threat of a bad object or the absence of a good but damaged one, but by the generous presence of the good object.

That it is the link and not only the object that is subjected to attacks has important consequences for our technique, as we need to be aware of the nuances of the emotional contact with the patient (Etchegoyen & Nemas, 2003). It is the realisation of the fragility of the link that needs to be protected from both members of the couple.

In our consulting rooms

Bion's emphasis on mental functioning could be understood as extensions of the linking functions of the human mind as well as of its difficulties and disturbances (Bianchedi, 1997).

In one of the last papers he wrote, "Making the best of a bad job" (1989[1979], p. 247), there is a much quoted phrase: "When two personalities meet, an emotional storm is created".

He goes on to say,

> One does not immediately know what the emotional storm is, but the problem is how to make the best of it, how to turn the adverse circumstance – as I choose to call it at the moment – to good account. (1989[1979], p. 247)

Bion's idea about what the emotional encounter is about goes beyond the objects involved but refers to what happens between them. As a result, we, as analysts, are deeply engaged in the depths of our minds in the emotional contact with our patients, taking into account transference and countertransference, projective identification, reverie function, and containment of the projected emotions to transform them into a communicable experience.

In our clinical work, Bion's description has opened up new territories. Although he initially referred to schizophrenic patients, we may find representations in the analysis of patients of every degree of disturbance: schizoid personalities, shallowness, narcissistic character traits, and many of the patients that populate our consulting rooms in these times.

My thoughts come out of my clinical experience with patients who present narcissistic personality disorders for whom the conceptual tool of attacks on linking might help understand the difficulties encountered in the development of the treatment and the nature of the countertransference.

Clinical material

I now reflect on the clinical material of a patient who was in treatment with me twenty years ago for five years and has now come back to see me. At the time I first saw her, I was not very familiar with Bion's ideas but, looking back, I think that her problems with relatedness can be understood as manifestations of her attacks on linking. Her difficulties in tolerating and sustaining links expressed themselves not only in her isolation, but also in her relation to her body, which she subjected to all types of manipulation to change its appearance.

Miss A first came to see me when she was thirty years old—a tall, sophisticated looking and attractive young woman who, despite her height, wore very high heels, which gave her the appearance of someone who looked at the world from above. Her way of carrying her very expensive coats evoked in me the image of the gods on Olympus in their chariots enveloped in clouds. She was—in her own words—very depressed and empty and, in the first interview, she cried all the time while talking without making any effort to dry her tears, as if she did not realise that they were running down her face and neck. Her days went by going from one place to the other in her car, without staying long anywhere, or watching television in the same zapping way. She had dropped out from university and had made some attempts at working that did not last long.

A is the eldest of four siblings, but she contends that she has always felt like an only child. Accordingly, she has never felt any jealousy towards her brother and sisters even though she has been told that she had tried to suffocate her little sister with a pillow and that she had tried to throw her baby brother out of his cot—stories which seemed to contradict her earlier statements.

A's parents divorced when she was eleven years old, both parents remarried and lived outside the country, and the children were brought up by the maternal grandparents. A has very conflictual relations with her mother when she comes to Argentina; otherwise, she keeps infrequent telephone contact with both parents.

In her adolescence, A was extremely preoccupied with her appearance; she saw herself as ugly and fat. The mother was considered an outstanding beauty and seemed to confirm A's fears about her own appearance as she supported and even encouraged her daughter in undergoing several plastic surgeries. A was never convinced that the surgeries had taken place; she felt cheated, as she could never recognise any changes in herself after they were performed.

A had a breakdown in her late adolescence. While she was boarding at an exclusive Swiss school, she undertook a journey with her grandmother to Egypt, where she felt that she had made an impressive impact on the men there, who offered to buy her. A was in a state of elation which then collapsed when she returned to the school, where she started taking laxatives and diuretics and had a severe episode of bulimia. She had to be taken back home.

By the time she started treatment, A was going out with a boy who belonged to the jet set. They were in a relationship of mutual ill treatment; she was not in love with him but she was afraid of feeling very isolated if she broke off the relationship and also of being excluded from his rich and powerful family.

A was a compulsive buyer and had to resort to very complicated manoeuvres to get rid of the clothes she did not wear any more. She never liked the clothes she had bought and, as soon as she bought them, she would take them to be restyled.

She came to see me prompted by a friend, Laura, the only one in her milieu who was in analysis. They seemed to share some traits, though Laura was the "successful" one, in a relationship with a rich businessman, following a university career, and had been a model. Miss A felt in her shadow.

The emotional atmosphere in the sessions

The degree of pessimism, despair, and devastation that A brought to the sessions led me constantly to try to rescue myself so as not to stay trapped in the apocalyptic view of the world proposed by the patient.

The world she described, a prolongation of her internal world, was populated by objects incapable of concern: egotistic and, at the same time, desperate. Trust could be sustained by A for only minutes at a time; to keep the analysis going I needed to turn to my own hopeful and patient internal objects to help me continue with her over the years. At other times, I was overwhelmed by feelings of futility in the face of her acting, the rigidity of character traits so shallow as to be close to stupidity, and her incapacity to develop intimate relationships that were not tainted by opportunistic strategies.

What A's internal resources were to be able to survive and establish some sort of—albeit distorted—relation with me was an interesting question. She would have a recurrent fantasy of falling ill with cancer and not following a treatment, or committing suicide in some distant place where nobody would find her.

I now present three dreams from different periods of her treatment.

Looting and weaning

> "I saw myself buying a lot of clothes with my mother; we already had two bags full. All of a sudden there was the end of the world or the end of humanity. I had to run away from a flat, taking with me a black bitch and a black mare. I was frenetically trying to put clothes in a bag and looked desperately for a jacket but could not find it. When I went out I realised that I was on the eighteenth floor, much higher than I had thought. People were trampling on each other."

The analysis of this dream allowed us to bring to light two situations that weighed heavily on my patient in the first year of analysis: the compulsive buying of clothes and the breast plastic surgery. A and Laura spent hours discussing which model was more beautiful and which one they would like to look like. This went together with detailed waist and bust measurements. Any variation in these measurements was accompanied by variations in the frame of mind of both friends. At one point, the two decided to undergo breast surgery, twice for A and three times for Laura, as they were not satisfied with the size obtained. These enactments were unstoppable and we could only reflect on them once they were done.

At the same time, and related to the material we were working on, her compulsive buying started appearing in the sessions, a fact that had been kept secret in the analysis until then. It was possible to relate this compulsion with her bulimic episodes in the past.

The compulsion to buy clothes, the old bulimic episodes, the dream, and the inevitability of the plastic surgery were related at that time to difficulties in a weaning which seemed to have had traumatic qualities for A in her internal world. The buying seemed to be related to a looting of the breast, keeping all the clothes for herself in two bags/breasts killed by the voracious attack. She responds by being herself two enormous breasts in order to elude dependence, but the breasts are artificial, they do not produce authentic food, leaving her again and again with a feeling of hunger and emptiness. The vicious circle that ensues can be understood by Bion's description of enforced splitting (1962, p. 10), the solution in order not to die: the baby relates to a breast that only yields physical nurture without love or understanding.

At the time, my preoccupations had to do with how this patient would be able to settle in the analytic relation and tolerate dependence on an analytic breast. I was not aware of the intolerance A felt about the link itself we would both develop. Looking back, I think that the prevailing shallowness and the acting out were expressions of the desire to annihilate the buds of a link that could begin to be established between her and me, with the risk of the outcome of a fruitful relation that would not be of her own doing. In this same sense, I think that the way she manipulated her body was the result of denying her origin in the intercourse of the parents in order to become her own creation.

The brands and the marks

> "We went with my mother, my grandmother, and my sister to New York. We were at a hairdresser, or in a changing room or a bathroom, it's not clear. Two women dressed as nurses came in, caught some women unaware and they ironed their faces with an iron, leaving a mark. It was something that produced unbearable pain. They did it to my sister but she seemed to endure it; she only looked perplexed. I could escape because I went from one place to the other, in and out, and although I realised what was going on I did not say a word. I even knew what they were up to, but all the same I said nothing."

The associations to this dream are difficult to translate into English because of the ambiguity of the words used.

A associated this dream with the branding of the cattle who do not understand what is happening to them and are also impotent. Other associations led to the world of fashion brands to which A was addicted. She sometimes bought things she did not like, but the brand was a guarantee that she belonged to the elite who wore that brand so she would not become an outcast. (The branding of cattle is *yerra* in Spanish, which also means "mistake".) She would collapse and even leave a place if she suspected that somebody was criticising her appearance. She used to wear clothes in which the brand was quite visible.

Other associations led us to a more complex configuration, that of the "marked people". A's way of communication took the form of projective identifications that were the spilling out of despair. She felt that people who got in contact with her remained marked. I could understand this way of communication and explore its consequences in my countertransference experience. As an example of this situation, a subject that came up with a certain frequency was that she was afraid that she had become pregnant and that she would have to undergo an abortion. This included the demand that I should direct her to a doctor to perform the abortion, with the veiled threat that should she have to find one herself, she would expose herself to danger and die. At the time, I understood this as her belief that I would become marked by her depression. In one of the sessions, she left behind her dark glasses on the couch, which reminded me of the black animals of the first dream, representing the dead breasts.

This was an attack on the linking functions that were in danger of developing in the analysis, which were attempting to question her omnipotence. As soon as something creative appeared in the session, even her own dreams, A wanted to involve me in the destruction of the creative link between the two of us that could result in the development of the capacity to think about herself and to be able to own her emotional experiences without automatic projection. Bonds were misunderstood by this aspect of her personality as the branding of the cattle; a submission to a tyrannical owner, a terrible persecuting internal character which Bion has called the ego-destructive superego. A wanted me to become associated with the abortionist, placing me in a cattle chute; a no-way-out situation from which I emerge marked.

At a crossroad: between the adolescent gang and the string quintet

> "I was in bed, in my room. I hear a lock being opened, like somebody trying to force the entrance door. Before that, somebody had rung the intercom; I hear many voices at the same time, I cannot understand the name. I go near the door and I hear a group of boys and girls going out of the elevator, talking. They are going to come into my flat. They are around twelve to thirteen years old and I suddenly realise that they are

taking over my house. I am afraid they will see me and I run to the stairs, frenzied. I tell the doorman what happened and he tells me that while I was away he had rented my flat and that he regretted it. He tries to kiss me and I run away, but I want him to call the police. I go back to the flat but now it's a terrace, not a flat, where a party is taking place. I go back downstairs to the street and I see my mother's dog. She is on her own; I know that my mother has left for Europe and I realise that she has forgotten the dog. I think about what to do and I decide to go to my grandmother's even if it's very far."

I shall refer to a session of the day before which I take as the counterpoint to this dream.

At the time of this dream, A is at the university and she is taking a course in art. The week before they had visited a museum where she saw adolescent children drawing, as the museum as it is also a school of art. It was beautiful seeing them. The day before the dream, they had the visit of a string quartet with performers from the Colón Theater. They spoke about the importance of the conductor, but she cannot find the word for it and refers to the teacher instead. She says that she was moved. The students were invited to take the baton and it was possible to see how something that seemed so easy was so difficult to do. I interpret that she seems to be valuing my conduct of this analysis as something that she can see as creative, as the picture/dreams of her mind, so we can think together in the session.

In recent sessions, A had been revising her ideas about the severity and relentless image of her father and we could relate those to the transference. I told her that if the analysis had been based on my severity and her submission to my interests, it was difficult to conceive how it would go on without those characteristics that seemed to support it.

Taking the dream and the material of recent sessions, there is an interesting crossroads at this more advanced point of the treatment, regarding a choice between two models, one related to manic defences and the other tentatively depressive. On the one hand, there is recognition of the creativity of the father, the conductor of the orchestra, with the baton that might stand for the setting and the interpretation, a difficult task recognised as such which has to respect the rhythms of growth as opposed to the taking into assault the body of the mother, as in the dream. On the other hand, there is a corrupt father/doorman who makes an alliance with the narcissistic pubertal gang that invades the mind and a terrace to organise a manic party in which the baby aspects are abandoned and forgotten.

Twenty years later

A came back to see me a few months ago, twenty years after having finished her five-year analytic treatment with me. Had I been too optimistic about her possibilities of choice in her development?

She is in her fifties now, her face modified by plastic surgeries, desperate about her hair loss, which seems to be her main complaint but which is not noticeable to an observer. She has been depressed since her grandmother's death, more than five years ago. She had looked after her grandmother, to whom she was very (ambivalently) attached and she had done it with devotion. She has been living with a man—a successful publisher—for almost twenty years. She also looked after him when he was ill some time ago. She lives in a flat that has been minutely decorated, but she does not feel comfortable in it. The kitchen is spotless; she would never cook in it and gets the food either from her mother's house or from restaurants. Her indolence is striking but she is very active in taking care of her mother's and partner's financial issues, which she does very well. Any small domestic difficulty is felt immediately as a tragedy, every wind a hurricane.

Interestingly enough, she came back to see me after many years; it is difficult to say why she has decided on this path. Manifestly, she wants me to help her get her mane back, as she feels she has lost an important part of her attractiveness. She has been told that her hair loss is a result of anxiety and stress, so it would only be reasonable to expect that the analysis would help her in this respect. She becomes impatient whenever I try to understand—or perhaps instil—some meaning in her hair loss.

She is now appalled at the changes she "inflicted" on her appearance through the plastic surgeries and other cosmetic interventions. Actually, her face changes impressively depending on her state of mind, and when she smiles she can be quite charming, but she sees herself as a "monster". I think that this monstrosity derives from her having attacked the parental coitus in order to fulfil a fantasy of auto gestation. It is difficult for her to accept love from her partner, as she wishes to be loved because of her beauty, not tolerating the love that comes from the object. She envies the capacity and the freedom of the object to love her.

The atmosphere in the sessions has changed noticeably; there are no traces of the old pseudo collaboration and her demands for my help are more overt, as well as her complaints about not receiving it. Just in passing, she said that she told her mother that I was a very good analyst but she would not accept being helped. At other times, she says that it is too late for her to change, but that she needs to come to the sessions to talk about her anxiety in a way that she cannot do anywhere else.

We are still struggling with the emotional turbulence of this new encounter, fluctuating between feelings of futility balanced only by the interest (K) and emotional responses that this patient evokes in me. She leads an impoverished life and it is not clear at all if the analysis could have helped her develop in other ways. As with other narcissistic patients who arrive at middle age, the mourning they have to face confronts them with what they feel is a lack of tools to work through it.

Between pessimism and realism

It is interesting to notice that "Envy and gratitude" (1975[1957]), as well as "Analysis terminable and interminable" (1937c), were written by Klein and Freud, respectively, in the last part of their work and of their lives. The authors refer to the factors that can negatively influence the outcome of an analysis. Both think that there is a bedrock which acts as a resistance to analysis, whether it comes from narcissism, the repetition compulsion, pathological splitting, or envy. This would account for the little efficacy of some analytic treatments in producing structural changes in the personalities. On the other hand, in her article, Klein holds the hope that the early and systematic interpretation of envy and its derivatives will be effective. Nevertheless, we also know that any attempt to interpret envy directly or naïvely are very rarely successful.

Bion, on the other hand, described the subtle mechanism of attacks on linking and on linking functions together with reversible perspective, transformation in hallucinosis, and other phenomena very early in his work in studying the psychotic part of the personality. Bion's investigation into thinking processes has been able to clarify two forms of mental functioning that reveal the complexity of the psychic structure and that extend from the neurotic to the psychotic pole. As Etchegoyen says (1991, p. 757), "Bion's work is the culmination of a sustained effort by Freud to integrate and delineate psychosis and neurosis which then reappears in Klein's theory of the positions". To speak of a psychotic personality does not imply a psychiatric diagnosis; the final outcome of the personality will depend on the mixture, interaction, and predominance of the neurotic or the psychotic aspect. The final outcome of this in/balance will determine the capacity for psychic change and psychic growth.

Some final reflections in another key

It has been said that nowadays we enjoy more individual freedom than ever before and yet our intimacy is much more susceptible to the influence of power and the market. What were once experiences in the solitude of the private sphere have become material for public debate, or are exhibited through social networks, reality shows, biographical books, or pornography. There seems to have been a displacement from introspection and regard for intimacy to hyperconnection without personal bondages. The past decades have seen a proliferation of media and artistic channels that "exhibit intimacy", which suggests a transformation of subjectivities and points to new ways of living and being in the world. What is the place for emotional links in our society and how does that affect our clinical work? Can we consider the current ways of being connected as misunderstandings, some kind of attack on intimate relations, or are they new forms of manifestations of human interactions?

More and more of our consulting hours are taken up by narcissistic or borderline patients who come to us with conscious or unconscious feelings of loneliness, emptiness, hollowness, or defences against these. The prevalence of sensuality over emotionality, drug addiction or symbiotic relations, psychosomatic illness, and feelings of inauthenticity, disillusions, and difficulties in sustaining meaningful relations are common features our patients present nowadays in the analysis.

What kinds of links are there present in these persons? Are the difficulties they present related to some form of attack on meaningful and creative linking functions, or is there a lack in their capacity to relate derived from other mechanisms? I believe these are some of the questions that challenge us in our current clinical practice.

References

Bianchedi, E. T. (1997). From objects to links: discovering relatedness. *Journal of Melanie Klein and Object Relations, 15*(2): 227–234.

Bion, W. R. (1962). *Learning from Experience.* London: Heinemann.

Bion, W. R. (1967)[1959]. Attacks on linking. In: *Second Thoughts* (pp. 93–110). New York; Jason Aronson.

Bion, W. R. (1989)[1979]. Making the best of a bad job. In: *Clinical Seminars and Four Papers* (pp. 247–257). Abingdon, Oxon: Fleetwood Press.

Etchegoyen, R. (1991). *The Fundamentals of Psychoanalytic Technique.* London: Karnac.

Etchegoyen, R., & Nemas, C. (2003). Salieri's dilemma: a counterpoint between envy and appreciation. *International Journal of Psychoanalysis, 84*: 45–58.

Freud, S. (1937c). Analysis terminable and interminable. *S. E., 23*: 211–253. London: Hogarth.

Klein, M. (1975)[1957]. Envy and gratitude. In: *Envy and Gratitude and Other Works. The Writings of Melanie Klein Vol III* (pp. 176–236). London: Hogarth Press and the Institute of Psychoanalysis, 1975.

Steuerman, E. (2000). *The Bounds of Reason.* London: Routledge.

CHAPTER THREE

Bion as a Kleinian: an elaboration of the phantasy of the mind in "Attacks on linking"

Rachel B. Blass

Reading Bion today

In recent years, much has been written about Bion's thinking, with authors widely differing on what is the essence of his contribution and what makes it valuable (e.g., Eigen, 1981; Ferro, 2005; Mawson, 2010; O'Shaughnessy, 2005; Sandler, 2010; Symington & Symington, 1996; Taylor, 2011; Vermote, 2011). This diversity might, in part, be a consequence of the complexity of his ideas and his peculiar and, at times, enigmatic way of writing. Undoubtedly, it is also related to the fact that, in his final years, his thinking radically changed. As may be seen from the title of his collected essays, *Second Thoughts,* and the reflections contained in its last chapter, Bion himself was quite aware of such changes and it was important for him to point them out to his readers. While some authors consider the heart of Bion's contribution to psychoanalysis to lie in his work prior to the change, others think that it is only with it that he dramatically innovates (see Blass, 2011a).

The shift that took place in Bion's later work is commonly thought to entail a departure from a traditional London Kleinian framework of thinking to something else. While there is much less consensus on what that "something else" is, two main ideas are often referred to in recent writing on Bion: one focuses on Bion's concern with desirable maternal care. According to this idea, Bion's thinking on "containment" implies a model of early psychological development and of pathology, which centres primarily on environmental deficit. It describes the mother's developmental task and the damage that ensues from her failure adequately to meet it. In turn, the analytic situation is regarded as a kind of corrective to real deficient mothering the patient had received during infancy, centred on a relationship in which the analyst takes over the missing maternal role of containment in an effort to correct the damage that its absence caused. Understood in this way, Bion resembles Winnicott in certain important respects, with the differences between Winnicott's "holding" and Bion's "containing" minimised (see Hamilton, 1996). At times, when portrayed like this, Bion seems as though he was a cognitive psychologist, concerned with helping and encouraging the patient to give words to experience—a capacity which has failed to adequately develop due to the deficient maternal environment. The other main idea regarding the change that is found in Bion's later work emphasises his concern with the "ineffable essence of being" and how the analytic situation opens one to it by putting aside all attempts at understanding the patient and all theoretical ideas on which such understanding is based (Vermote, 2011). Instead of understanding on the part of both analyst and patient, what is needed is some special kind of spontaneous presence that opens one to one's very existence (de Bianchedi, 2005; Ferro, 2005). This idea is thought to be encompassed in Bion's reflections on O. These ideas clearly radically depart from a traditional Kleinian approach and what it considers essential to psychoanalysis: unconscious phantasy and its interpretation in the analytic encounter through maintaining a neutral analytic stance which allows for understanding of transference and projective identification and which ultimately leads to integration of split off parts of the self (Klein, 1975).

The view that Bion's important contributions should be seen in terms of ideas on "maternal care" and "openness to experience" has become increasingly popular. This may be tied in part to an effort to validate newer American relational and intersubjective theories. By reading what is essential and valuable in Bion in this way, the newer theories can maintain that their thinking, while innovative, is in line with traditional psychoanalysis and naturally emerges from it since they are following in the footsteps of Bion, who was a leading figure in the traditional analytic group of London Kleinians (e.g., Greenberg, 1994; Levine, 2000, p. 971). Moreover, the newer theories can argue that in developing their relational ideas they have not overlooked, but, rather, have incorporated, the relational contributions that were introduced by that group. The popularity of such readings of Bion could also be tied to the desire to expand the scope of psychoanalysis so that it will include mystical ideas and spiritual stances which, in recent years, have been gaining popularity in the broader society (Lasch, 1990).

The growing emphasis on the importance of Bion's later thinking may downplay or blur Bion's important contributions to the foundations of traditional Kleinian thinking and practice. Alternatively, those foundations might become blurred, reinterpreted in the light of what are considered to be Bion's newer ideas. Moreover, the popularity of Bion that has followed the expansion of the scope of his ideas and the fact that he was consequently adopted by a wide range of schools seems to have resulted in a situation in which, at times, basic Kleinian or Freudian ideas are regarded as Bionian innovations. For example, Bion tends to be regarded as the analyst who developed the notions of epistemophilia and a theory of thinking, while these are actually well grounded both in Freud and in Klein (Blass, 2006).

In the light of all this, I find special value today in studying Bion as a Kleinian. That is, I think it is important to consider Bion's important place within traditional Kleinian thinking, to appreciate where his contribution is thought to lie from a London Kleinian perspective. While undoubtedly Bion's later work diverges from that of a traditional Kleinian approach, this should not overshadow (or, conversely, exaggerate) what he added to traditional analytic thought and practice.

To consider Bion as a Kleinian, he must be regarded in context. It is when seen in the light of certain fundamental dimensions of Klein's thinking that his significance to her approach best comes to the fore. In what follows, I first describe these dimensions of Klein's thinking and then turn to Bion's contribution, focusing on his "Attacks on linking".

The Kleinian context of Bion's contribution[1]

What then are the essential and foundational dimensions of Klein's work that need to be taken into account to appreciate Bion's contribution? One way of addressing this question is by examining what distinguishes her work from Freud's. In this context it is possible to speak of the very influential ideas Klein introduced regarding early development, its different phases, and the roles of destructiveness and of projective identification. However, in and of themselves these ideas seem to merely add themes (e.g., pre-oedipal ones to Freud's oedipal ones), not to significantly affect how we regard human nature and the analytic process and thus it is difficult to see them as defining Klein's analytic approach. Some have suggested that the differentiating and defining dimension of Klein's work is her relational focus relative to Freud's biological, individualistic, abstract, and metapsychological ones (de Bianchedi et al., 1988). But such divisions are very general and ultimately are untenable. One can see that Klein herself recognised this. For example, on the primal nature of object relations she writes that

> the difference between Freud's view and my own is less wide than appears at first sight . . . In various contexts he explicitly and implicitly expressed opinions which suggested a relation to an object, the mother's breast, preceding auto-erotism and narcissism. (1952, p. 435)

She goes on to cite Freud (one of his Encylopaedia articles, 1923a, pp. 235–254) on how autoerotism is a displacement of an attachment to the breast. And then, referring to the *Ego and the Id* (Freud, 1923b), states that

> Freud then defines the first and most important identifications which lie hidden behind the ego-ideal as the identification with the father, or with the parents, and places them, as he expresses it, in the "pre-history of every person". These formulations come close to what I described as the first introjected objects. (1952, p. 435)

And while it might be argued that the nature of Klein's concerns with transference, the analytic relationship and the interpretation of unconscious contents distinguishes her approach from Freud's on the level of technique, here, too, the common ground between the two is considerable (Blass, 2011b; Strachey, 1934).

Indeed, Klein is distinguished from Freud by the emphases she puts on certain aspects of his thinking and practice and the downplaying of others, as well as by her addition of themes (phantasies, defences, and phases). However, in my view, the unique contribution of her thinking is more dramatic and has a more dramatic impact on the nature of analytic work. This has to do with her way of thinking about unconscious phantasy. It is in regard to her thinking on phantasy that Bion's contribution becomes most apparent.

Unconscious phantasy

In a recent study of the relationship between Freud and Klein (Blass, 2014) I have argued that one major feature that characterises Klein's notion of phantasy and distinguishes it from Freud's is that, according to Klein's notion, phantasies are considered to be the basic building blocks of our mind (Isaacs, 1991[1943]). Phantasies about objects and about the relationships between them are not merely thoughts entertained *in* our minds that affect how we feel and act, but, rather, they are the material of the ego and of the mind itself. That is, changes in our phantasies have a direct and concrete impact on our states of mind. This position is based on two foundational ideas: first, that I and my objects are me. For example, in my relationship with a maternal object in my inner world, both myself and the maternal object are parts of myself and are composed of various parts of myself. The second idea is that my objects *are* my mind. Thus, if, in my phantasy, I have attacked the maternal object, not only is part of myself under attack, but also part of my mind could be damaged.

Freud, on the other hand, tends to focus on internal phantasies about the actions and thoughts of objects that are experienced as more distinct from us, from ourselves. They are more like internal representatives of external objects or distinct or, perhaps, alien agents within us ("others"). Consequently, for him, our state of mind is a response to what *we* imagine an internal object would do or feel *in response* to our wishes and is less a direct derivative of what we feel towards the object. In the infant's mind, according to Freud, the internal object (and later the superego) may withdraw love and never return if the infant is sadistic (but it is not that the sadism itself entails the object's destruction). Indeed, for Freud, too, our minds are made up of internal and internalised relationships and, like Freud, Klein is concerned with our phantasies regarding the possible reaction of the object. But there is, nevertheless, an important qualitative difference.[2]

In Isaacs' "The nature and function of phantasy", the connection between phantasy and the state of one's mind is most clearly described. In the first published version of that paper, Isaacs writes, "'mere' beliefs about internal objects . . . lead to real effects . . . profound changes in the ego character and personality" (Isaacs, 1948, p. 92), and she explains that the effects pertain to the very capacity to think:

> *when the child feels he has dismembered his mother, his mental life is split and disintegrated* – he shows the most acute anxiety, he is confused and behaves chaotically, he cannot see or hear or control what he does and says, and so on. It is not that, *first*, his mental life becomes disintegrated and he *then* interprets this as having dismembered his mother; it is *because he wants to* dismember his mother, intends to, tries to and in imagination does so, that he feels his own ego to be split and disintegrated, and shows in his behaviour that "mental disintegration" which we can describe and label and talk about.
>
> We, for our purpose of comparing one mind with another and making generalizations, can see what happens to the child, the way he behaves, and can describe it as "mental disintegration". But the child experiences it as "my-mother-inside-me-is-in bits". (Isaacs, 1991[1943], pp. 275–276)

In other words, our phantasies about objects affect our feelings, our behaviour, our ego, but also the very mind in which they (in phantasy) exist. Klein writes,

> I believe that the ego is incapable of splitting the object—internal and external—without a corresponding splitting taking place within the ego. Therefore the phantasies and feelings about the state of the internal object vitally influence the structure of the ego. The more sadism prevails in the process of incorporating the object, and the more the object is felt to be in pieces, the more the ego is in danger of being split in relation to the internalized object fragments.
>
> The processes I have described are, of course, bound up with the infant's phantasy-life; and the anxieties which stimulate the mechanism of splitting are also of a phantastic nature. It is in phantasy that the infant splits the object and the self, but the effect of this phantasy is a very real one, because it leads to feelings and relations (and later on, thought-processes) being in fact cut off from one another. (1975[1946], p. 6)

She adds, "The various ways of splitting the ego and internal objects result in the feeling that the ego is in bits. This feeling amounts to a state of disintegration" (1975[1946], p. 10).

Klein's introduction of the concept of "projective identification", which centres on the phantasy of putting parts of oneself in the other, is intimately tied to these ideas. In describing this process, Klein explains that

> As far as the ego is concerned the excessive splitting off and expelling into the outer world of parts of itself considerably weaken it. For the [projected] aggressive component of feelings and of the personality is intimately bound up in the mind with power, potency, strength, knowledge and many other desired qualities. (1975[1946], p. 8)

With excessive projection of good parts, "good parts of the personality are felt to be lost, and in this way the mother becomes the ego-ideal; this process too results in weakening and impoverishing the ego. (1975[1946], p. 9).

While, in this context, Klein speaks of the impact on the ego, the ego for Klein (as for Freud) is also the seat of mental functioning (Blass, 2012). That is why "the ego is in bits . . . amounts to a state of disintegration".

Klein's perspective on phantasy has a major impact not only on the understanding of the person, but also on the analytic situation. Klein, like Freud, is concerned to elucidate phantasy through the interpretation of transference. But what Klein adds to Freud regarding the meaning of phantasy changes what this involves. The analyst in the transference is seen not only in terms of projected objects and the patient's phantasied relationship with them. Rather, the analyst is seen in terms of projected parts of the self. That is, the analyst is attuned not only to how he is made to fit into the patient's unconscious relational story, how that relational truth comes alive in the analytic situation, but to how that story is about relationships within the patient's *mind* and is lived out through the phantasied impact on the analyst (putting parts of the self into him, controlling him, merging with him). The story is also about the patient's lived experience of the fact that the analyst does *not* neatly fit into the patient's relational story: the analyst has a mind of his own. This experience might be both painful and desired.

This more focused concern with the mind would mean, for example, alongside thinking, "Who am I in the transference?", the analyst will be concerned with which part of the patient's mind the patient is (in phantasy) putting into the analyst and how that is affecting the patient's thinking.

Bion's elaborations of Kleinian phantasy in "Attacks on linking"

The phantasy of "Attacks on linking"

In "Attacks on linking", Bion articulates a very central phantasy that adds in a significant way to Klein's ideas on phantasy and thinking. Here lies one of his major contributions to the traditional Kleinian approach. What is striking in this phantasy, and especially innovative, is that it is focused directly on the mind. That is, the phantasy is not so much about objects that constitute the mind and, thus, directly impact upon the functioning of the mind (one's own and others); rather, the phantasy is of the mind itself. Just as there are phantasies about the mother or her breast, there are, Bion suggests, phantasies about the mind, about the way we think. And while other leading Kleinians, most notably Herbert Rosenfeld and Hanna Segal, take a similar step at about the same time that Bion does, Bion most clearly puts this new idea on the table and makes it the heart of analytic work.

In "Attacks on linking", the phantasy of the mind centres on one major image of it. This is the image of the mind as a connecting force, a kind of mechanism whose function is to bring together, *to link*, thoughts, ideas, and feelings. The use of the verb "to link" here is significant. Relative to other verbs that express the act of connecting, it emphasises the distinctness of the joined parts (in contrast, for example, to "to unite") and yet their having a natural tendency to come together into a larger unit (like links in a chain). It also strongly connotes an act of connecting that is both communicative (as in a satellite link) and physical (as in "linking arms"). In fact, the meaning of the verb "link" in its Middle English origin was "to physically connect".

Indeed, in Bion's elaboration of the phantasy, it is clear that the mind and its functions are regarded as very physical and emotional. Bion states that "The prototype for all the links of which I wish to speak is the primitive breast or penis" (1959, p. 308). He explicitly refers the reader to Klein and her view of phantasy, projective identification, and the Oedipus complex, emphasising that his addition will be in connecting her view of the phantasy of attacking the breast to the more general phantasy of attacking that which creatively links between objects and between ideas and feelings in a way that allows for meaningful and emotionally connected thinking (in contrast to thinking that is merely logical, mathematical, and sterile, (p. 315)).

Interestingly, Bion notes that he already discussed these ideas in "Differentiation of the psychotic from the non-psychotic personalities" and here is merely further illustrating them. This is true, and points to the power of the very concept of "Attacks on linking". It creates such a dominant image, which in itself so strongly describes a foundational phantasy, that one tends to associate the phantasy not with its first serious elaboration in Bion's writings, but with the paper that comes under the title of "Attacks on linking". It were as though the title itself so captures the essence of the phenomenon it comes to describe that little more about it needs to be said. The fact is, however, that Bion's elaborations of the phantasy are important both in "Differentiation of the psychotic from the non-psychotic personalites" and in "Attacks on linking". I turn now to the former.

Attacks on linking in the "Differentiation of the psychotic from the non-psychotic personalities" (from Freud to Klein)

In "Differentiation of the psychotic from the non-psychotic personalities", Bion's effort to understand the thinking of the psychotic first leads him back to the Freudian roots of the "attacks on linking" phantasy. These are to be found in Freud's view that, in psychosis, the ego withdraws itself from a part of reality that is disturbing. Bion explains that this withdrawal is, in fact, a destructive phantasy, which (in accordance with the Kleinian view of phantasy) has a real effect on the mind. He writes,

> the withdrawal from reality is an illusion, not a fact, and arises from the deployment of projective identification against the mental apparatus listed by Freud. Such is the dominance of this phantasy that it is evident that it is no phantasy, but a fact, to the patient, who acts as if his perceptual apparatus could be split into minute fragments and projected into his objects. (1957, p. 267)

Next, Bion ties this phantasy of destruction of reality to Klein's phantasies of sadistic attacks on the breast. Here, it becomes clear, however, that, for Bion, the central aim of the attacks is not the destruction of the object *per se*, but of the mind itself. "The psychotic," he states, "splits his objects, and contemporaneously all that part of his personality, which would make him aware of the reality he hates, into exceedingly minute fragments" (Bion, 1957, p. 268). It is after describing how this fragmentation affects the psychotic's experience of reality that Bion introduces his new notion of linking and phantasy of attacks on linking. He writes,

> If we consider that one of the patient's objects in using splitting and projective identification is to rid himself of awareness of reality it is clear that he could achieve the maximum of severance from reality with the greatest economy of effort if he could launch these destructive attacks on the link, whatever it is, that connects sense impressions with consciousness. (p. 268)

He continues, "Not only is primitive thought attacked because it links sense-impressions of reality with consciousness but, thanks to the psychotic's over-endowment with destructiveness, the splitting processes are extended to the links within the thought processes themselves" (p. 269).

In other words, in introducing the notion of "attacks on linking", Bion offers a Kleinian reading of the process of withdrawal from reality that, according to Freud, characterised the psychotic's way of being. Its Kleinian nature can be seen in the shift from the description of withdrawal as a kind a cognitive process or defence mechanism to a description of it as a phantasy in which a motivated agent instigates an attack on its victim. The Kleinian nature of Bion's reading can also be seen in the fact that the destructive phantasy has an immediate impact on the state of the mind, on mental functioning. But it is only when we come to consider how and why it has its effect on the mind that Bion's important innovation comes to the fore. Here, it can be seen that the destructive phantasy that concerns Bion has an impact on the mind not because the mind comprises objects (e.g., the mother, the breast) that are damaged by the attack; rather, the impact on the mind is because the mind itself is what is attacked. That is, in this case, it is not that the "mother is in bits" and the mind, therefore, is disintegrated (as Isaacs, following Klein, suggested). Rather, more simply, the mind—having been subject to attack—is in bits. In other words, Bion's notion of "attacks on linking" makes very explicit the idea that we have inner phantasies not only of people, body parts, our self, and our ego, but of the thinking mind itself and of the processes of thought that go on in it.

The elaboration of the phantasy in "Attacks on linking" (clinical illustration and early notions of containment)

The paper "Attacks on linking" is written with the intention of bringing out the significance of this development in regard to phantasy and Bion does so in two main ways: (i) with the help of extensive clinical illustration of the different ways in which links can be attacked and (ii) through the introduction of the idea of containment which emerges from it.

Clinical illustration

As noted earlier, "Attacks on linking" begins with a statement by Bion that his thinking is grounded in Klein's ideas on early phantasy, splitting, projective identification, and the Oedipus complex (Bion, 1959, p. 308). Following this, he explains that since the analyst's role depends on linking through verbal communication, the phantasy of attacking the link, which he will address in this paper, is most accessible in the analytic situation. He then proceeds to demonstrate this with a long series of examples.

For instance, he describes a patient who, after thirty minutes of stating a series of facts about the world, apparently to try to maintain contact with reality, says that the analyst, Bion, would not understand him. Bion, in response, interprets the patient's feeling that he (Bion) does not want to take in what the patient wishes to deposit in him. All this seems covered by regular Kleinian thinking about projective identification. But then there is a shift in the description. The patient responds to Bion's interpretation by saying that there were "two probability clouds in the room". Bion takes this to be a reflection of the patient on the reality of his thinking. The patient, according to Bion, wonders whether what he experiences as Bion's badness is a fact or whether he, the patient, is hallucinating. Moreover, he wonders about this because he knows of his own envy and hatred of the analyst's capacity to understand.

It can be seen that what Bion is suggesting here is that the patient's relationship to the analyst's thinking, to his understanding (in this case, a relationship of hatred), is what determines his relationship to the analyst (his view of him as bad). This illustration highlights the novelty of Bion's thinking. Earlier, we saw how Isaacs introduced the idea that an attack on the object is not the consequence of mental disintegration (some form of cognitive breakdown), but the cause of it. That is, psychoanalysis explains our mental state in terms of phantasy, not unmotivated cognitive events. Here, Bion advances the idea that the attack on the object is indeed to be regarded as a consequence, not a cause, but it is a consequence not of mental disintegration, but of an attack on the mind, a motivated phantasied act of destruction directed towards the analyst's thought processes.

In the other examples that Bion offers, he presents a range of ways in which the linking aspects of thought processes are, in phantasy, directly damaged. Stammering prevents the use of language that could bond the patient and analyst. Sleep is a state of uncontrolled projective identification, which is a destructive attack on the coupling parents. Fragmenting what is visually seen in phantasy prevents "the parental intercourse state of mind" that is involved in thinking. Creative understanding is regarded "with hate and transformed into a hostile and destructive sexuality rendering the patient–analyst couple sterile" (p. 310). The analyst is perceived as one who opposes communication through rejection of projective identification. Judgement can then become alienated and, thus, its guidance rendered untrustworthy, experienced as an enigmatic and intimidating breast, as in the case of the probability clouds. The creative thinking that goes on between patient and analyst can come to be envied.

It is important to emphasise that while in these clinical descriptions Bion tends to speak of the mind as an object, his focus in these descriptions of the attacks on linking is on the mind as a function. He writes,

> I employ the term "link" because I wish to discuss the patient's relationship with a function rather than with the object that subserves a function; my concern is not only with the breast, or penis, or verbal thought, but with their function of providing the link between two objects. (p. 312)

Early notions of containment

Bion's focus on the linking function leads him to another powerful phantasy which emerges in this seminal paper—that of containment. While the phantasy of containment is only very partially developed in the present paper and must await the appearance of *Learning from Experience* (1962) until its complete exposition, its mention here is significant. It highlights the connection between Bion's thinking on "attacks on linking" and on "containment". By containment, Bion, at this point, refers to the phantasy that through projective identification painful or unthinkable parts of oneself are deposited in the mind of the object, are modified there, and are then returned in a way that makes those parts tolerable and thinkable. In one important variant of this phantasy, the object is felt to refuse the deposit of the projected parts or to quickly and, perhaps, aggressively evacuate them.

Careful study of the text reveals that Bion regards containment as a phantasy about one kind of process of linking that allows for thinking to take place. It is—like the phantasies about other kinds of linking processes that Bion refers to (e.g., the joining of disparate ideas)—a phantasy about a cognitive reality. However, in the discussion of containment, reality seems to takes on special significance. This is because, specifically in relation to containment, Bion turns to elucidate the early infant–mother relationship that underlies it. He writes,

> The analytic situation built up in my mind a sense of witnessing an extremely early scene. I felt that the patient had experienced in infancy a mother who dutifully responded to the infant's emotional displays. The dutiful response had in it an element of impatient "I don't know what's the matter with the child." My deduction was that in order to understand what the child wanted the mother should have treated the infant's cry as more than a demand for her presence. From the infant's point of view she should have taken into her, and thus experienced, the fear that the child was dying. It was this fear that the child could not contain. He strove to split it off together with the part of the personality in which it lay and project it into the mother. An understanding mother is able to experience the feeling of dread, that this baby was striving to deal with by projective identification, and yet retain a balanced outlook. This patient had had to deal with a mother who could not tolerate experiencing such feelings and reacted either by denying them ingress, or alternatively by becoming a prey to the anxiety which resulted from introjection of the infant's feelings. The

latter reaction must, I think, have been rare: denial was dominant. (Bion, 1959, p. 313)

Here, Bion might seem to be adopting a model of pathology based on environmental deficit. He might seem to be affirming that pathological states of mind emerge directly from the actual absence of proper mothering and, moreover, that tolerance of experience, more than understanding *per se*, is what proper mothering entails. Viewed in this way, Bion seems to be advancing (already at this relatively early point in his writing) the kind of models that the newer readings of Bion regard as his most important contributions. However, two things should be taken into account in this context. First, Bion thought that the environmental dimensions he referred to were to be regarded as additions to his main phantasy-orientated model. He writes,

> On the one hand there is the patient's inborn disposition to excessive destructiveness, hatred, and envy: on the other the environment which, at its worst, denies to the patient the use of the mechanisms of splitting and projective identification. On some occasions the destructive attacks on the link between patient and environment, or between different aspects of the patient's personality, have their origin in the patient; on others, in the mother, although in the latter instance and in psychotic patients, it can never be in the mother alone. (Bion, 1959, p. 313)

The mother is never a direct cause of pathology. The inner world is.

The second thing that needs to be taken into account is that Bion emphasises that the environmental need in this case is for understanding in the sense of linking ideas through verbal communication—this is the heart of "Attacks on linking". Since offering understanding of this kind is what Kleinian analysts have *always* regarded as the heart of the analytic method, the fact that Bion considers the patient's situation in terms of such a real environmental need does not affect the analyst's role. His thinking here does not in any way imply that the analyst should fulfil deficits through non-analytic dimensions of maternal care. What it implies, rather, is that the analyst should interpret with sensitivity to what understanding could mean to the patient in his inner world.

Bion's focus in his paper on attacks on understanding applies to the understanding that comes from containment as well. His elaborations in this regard are helpful. He explains that early denial of the infant's projective identification (whether its source is in the mother or the infant) leads to a destruction of the link between infant and breast that severely limits the desire and ability to think and learn. Moreover, out of envy and greed, there can develop phantasies of the object's reluctance to contain the object's projections even when this is not the case (e.g., when the analyst does, in fact, contain the projections). Or the breast can be felt to be greedy and willing to take in the projections only in order to destroy them—a dynamic that may be found in the belief of some patients that the analyst strives to understand them in order to drive them insane.

In all these dynamics, the tie between the breast and the mind is strong. It is a thinking breast that the patient seeks in his acts of projective identification and it is a thinking breast which is attacked in face of experienced failure of these acts.[3]

Concluding thoughts

I have argued that the Kleinian tradition is defined by a very specific notion of phantasy. It holds that our mind *is* our objects and, thus, what we phantasise in regard to our objects (e.g., chopping them up, projecting them) has an immediate impact on our thinking. Accordingly, Klein and her followers elaborated a range of phantasies and discussed their potential impact on our ability to think and know. Bion took this idea one important step further. Not only do our phantasied objects comprise our minds and have an impact on our thinking, but we have phantasies that pertain directly to our minds and thinking. Our minds and their functions are, too, in a sense, the objects of phantasy. Thinking can be desired, envied, hated, and, as "Attacks on linking" emphasises, attacked with very detrimental effects on one's ability to think.

In his elaboration of this phantasy, Bion fleshes out (literally, too) our understanding of thinking. He emphasises that it requires a linking of ideas and emotions and a creative joining of disparate ideas in an oedipal kind of union. Yet, at certain times, it also involves a specific maternal stance; the mother and then, later, the analyst must be able to contain—to introject, modify, and return—unbearable feelings projected into them. As we have seen, Bion explains that this maternal stance is *actually* needed in the course of the child's development in order for his thinking to evolve. But this concern with an actual environmental factor—at least at this point in his thinking—does not detract from his concern with phantasy (e.g., maternal understanding is the breast), and neither does it transform the analyst's role, which remains the traditional Kleinian one of understanding phantasy and interpreting it. Rather, Bion's elaboration of the actual processes involved in containment, as described in his "Attacks on linking", deepens our understanding of the lived meanings of understanding and of interpretation, of the deep dynamic forces and qualities of experience that they involve.

Over the years, other leading Kleinian analysts have developed Klein's notion of phantasy along similar lines, focusing specifically on the phantasy of the mind and of the processes of thought. For example, this is very apparent in the work of Hanna Segal on the phantasy of unlimited projective identification as a kind of unrestrained mental intercourse (Segal, 1997), of Herbert Rosenfeld on the communicative aspects of projective identification (Rosenfeld, 1988) and of Betty Joseph on the patient's attacks on understanding (Joseph, 1983). Bion's "Attacks on linking" is a contribution of vital importance for clearly articulating this development, elaborating it and making it so central to traditional Kleinian psychoanalysis.

Notes

1. This section and the next one contain descriptions of what is essential to Klein's thinking that I have put forth elsewhere (especially Blass, 2014).
2. To further clarify this point, one may note here that Freud allows for our phantasies to shape who we are and how we think through processes of identification (e.g., with an ideal object in narcissism, with an aggressive one in depression). However, in Freud, there is a clearer distinction than in Klein between myself and the other with whom I am identified. The aggressive object with whom part of me is identified is not really me. His idea of identification, in itself, implies the distinction. Similarly, in Freud, when one phantasises expelling from oneself all that is bad (Freud, 1925h, p. 237), the bad is usually expelled into the external world in such a way that an external—not internal—object is perceived as the source of danger

(as in phobias). In contrast, Klein would tend to speak of the badness being expelled into the internal object, which then immediately damages the self. Perhaps Freud comes closer to the notion of the immediacy of the impact of the phantasy on the mind in some descriptions of the relations between the ego and the superego, but, in general in his writings, we see that the wish to be rid of what is bad becomes a fear of an external object rather than the presence in the mind of a bad one.

3. It should be noted here that, in his later writing on containment, Bion seems to develop it so that it comes to relate to an additional phantasy regarding thinking, that of thinking as a digestive process.

References

Bion, W. R. (1957). Differentiation of the psychotic from the non-psychotic personalities. *International Journal of Psychoanalysis, 38*: 266–275.

Bion, W. R. (1959). Attacks on linking. *International Journal of Psychoanalysis, 40*: 308–315.

Bion, W. R. (1962). *Learning from Experience*. London: Tavistock.

Blass, R. B. (2006). A psychoanalytic understanding of the desire for knowledge as reflected in Freud's *Leonardo da Vinci and a Memory of his Childhood. International Journal of Psychoanalysis, 87*: 1259–1276.

Blass, R. B. (2011a). Introduction to "On the value of 'Late Bion' to analytic theory and practice". *International Journal of Psychoanalysis, 92*: 1081–1088.

Blass, R. B. (2011b). On the immediacy of unconscious truth: understanding Betty Joseph's 'Here and Now' through comparison with alternative views of it outside of and within Kleinian thinking. *International Journal of Psychoanalysis, 92*: 1137–1157.

Blass, R. B. (2012). The ego according to Klein: return to Freud and beyond. *International Journal of Psychoanalysis, 93*: 151–166.

Blass, R. B. (2014). On 'The Fear of Death' as the primary anxiety: how and why Klein differs from Freud. *International Journal of Psychoanalysis, 95*: 613–627.

De Bianchedi, E. T. (2005). Whose Bion? Who is Bion? *International Journal of Psychoanalysis, 86*: 1529–1534.

De Bianchedi, E. T., Scalozub de Boschan, L., de Cortiñas, L. P., & de Piccolo, E. G. (1988). Theories on anxiety in Freud and Melanie Klein: their metapsychological status. *International Journal of Psychoanalysis, 69*: 359–368.

Eigen, M. (1981). The area of faith in Winnicott, Lacan and Bion. *International Journal of Psychoanalysis, 62*: 413–433.

Ferro, A. (2005). Bion: theoretical and clinical observations. *International Journal of Psychoanalysis, 86*: 1535–1542.

Freud, S. (1923a). Two encyclopaedia articles. *S. E., 18*: 233–260. London: Hogarth.

Freud, S. (1923b). *The Ego and the Id. S. E., 19*: 3–66. London: Hogarth.

Freud, S. (1925h). Negation. *S. E., 19*: 233–240. London: Hogarth.

Greenberg, J. (1994). The changing paradigm of psychoanalysis. *International Forum of Psychoanalysis, 3*: 221–226.

Hamilton, V. (1996). *The Analyst's Preconscious*. Hillsdale, NJ: Analytic Press.

Isaacs, S. (1948). The nature and function of phantasy. *International Journal of Psychoanalysis, 29*: 73–97.

Isaacs, S. (1991)[1943]. The nature and function of phantasy In: P. King & R. Steiner (Eds.), *The Freud–Klein Controversies 1941–45* (pp. 264–321). London: Routledge.

Joseph, B. (1983). On understanding and not understanding: some technical issues. *International Journal of Psychoanalysis, 64*: 291–298.

Klein, M. (1952). The origins of transference. *International Journal of Psychoanalysis, 33*: 433–438.

Klein, M. (1975). *Envy and Gratitude and Other Works – 1946–1963*. London: Hogarth.

Klein, M. (1975)[1946]. Notes on some schizoid mechanisms. In: M. Klein, *Envy and Gratitude and Other Works – 1946–1963* (pp. 1–24). London: Hogarth.

Lasch, C. (1991). Afterword: The culture of narcissism revisited. In: *The Culture of Narcissism: American Life in an Age of Diminishing Expectation* (pp. 237–250). New York: W. W. Norton.

Levine, H. B. (2000). *Standing in the Spaces: Essays on Clinical Process, Trauma, and Dissociation: Phillip M. Bromberg*. Hillsdale NJ: Analytic Press.

Mawson, C. (Ed.) (2010). *Bion Today*. Hove: Brunner-Routledge.

O'Shaughnessy, E. (2005). Whose Bion? *International Journal of Psychoanalysis, 86*: 1523–1528.

Rosenfeld, H. (1988). Contribution to the psychopathology of psychotic states: the importance of projective identification in the ego structure and object relations of the psychotic patient. In: E. B. Spillius (Ed.), *Melanie Klein Today: Vol. 1—Mainly Theory* (pp. 117–137). London: Routledge.

Sandler, P. C. (2010). *The Language of Bion: A Dictionary of Concepts*. London: Karnac.

Segal, H. (1997). Changing models of the mind. In: C. Bronstein (Ed.), *Kleinian Theory. A Contemporary Perspective* (pp. 157–164). London: Whurr.

Strachey, J. (1934). The nature of the therapeutic action of psychoanalysis. *International Journal of Psychoanalysis, 15*: 127–159.

Symington, J., & Symington, N. (1996). *The Clinical Thinking of Wilfred Bion*. London: Routledge.

Taylor, D. (2011). Commentary on Vermote's "On the value of 'Late Bion' to analytic theory and practice". *International Journal of Psychoanalysis, 92*: 1099–1112.

Vermote, R. (2011). On the value of 'Late Bion' to analytic theory and practice. *International Journal of Psychoanalysis, 92*: 1089–1098.

CHAPTER FOUR

The sane and the insane psychotic: "Attacks on linking" revisited from Bion's later work

Rudi Vermote

Introduction

In *Second Thoughts* (1967a), Bion offered a commentary on his papers on psychosis from the 1950s ten years later. Along the same lines, it might be a valuable exercise to look at "Attacks on linking" from the perspective of his later theoretical work and clinical insights. I begin by summarising the core ideas of "Attacks on linking" (Bion, 1967d), then consider the paper in the light of some of his later concepts. I discuss Bion's technique at the time as reflected in the clinical material of the paper, and go on to discuss the relation between the obstructive object and omnipotent phantasy in psychosis which is prominent in the paper. This will lead us to Bion's view of the relation of the psychotic with the infinite and O, and his interesting idea about the difference between a sane and an insane psychotic. Finally, I discuss the way in which the phenomenon of attacks on linking differs in relation to transformations in O and in K, concluding with a more personal point of view on attacks on linking from perspective of a model of psychic functioning mainly based on Bion's work.

Bion's early ideas on psychosis as reflected in the "Attacks on linking" paper

The psychosis papers of the 1950s led to Bion's seminal "Theory of thinking" paper (Bion, 1967e). They reveal something of Bion's genius in bringing about a change in psychoanalytic technique and understanding by directing interventions from psychic content to psychic functioning. In order to enhance this psychic processing, Bion developed a kind of psychoanalytic–epistemological model for the practising psychoanalyst who deals with severe psychopathology.

In "Attacks on linking", we see how Bion begins from a Kleinian approach based on projective identification, splitting, envious attacks on the creative couple, and the breast and then gradually develops far-reaching original insights. He proposes that psychosis can be understood not as a manifestation of the debris left after a catastrophe, but, rather, as a sign of a continuous attack on mental functioning, which takes place in such a sustained and intensive way that even dreaming is no longer possible. These attacks give rise to evacuation of parts of the ego, so that seeing, hearing, and smelling are experienced in part as hallucinations. Psychic processing is fragmented by the attacks. Furthermore, Bion had the idea or intuition that there must be a relationship between the ongoing present catastrophe and a primary traumatic problem. In "Attacks on linking", Bion (1967d) relates this primary trauma to witnessing parental intercourse. He gives no evidence for this; it is a Kleinian preconception. In his paper "The imaginary twin" (Bion, 1967b), he also links the development of sight with the oedipal situation.

This is a hypothesis about the content; Bion's hypothesis that the early trauma consists of a failure of normal projective identification with the mother or carer is more important. This is not a theory about the content of the early trauma but about the ongoing default in psychic functioning. Bion saw projective identification not as a defence, but as the first form of communication. In this regard, he gives a first definition of containment in "Attacks on linking": "An understanding mother is able to experience the feeling of dread, that this baby was striving to deal with by projective identification, and yet retain a balanced outlook" (Bion, 1967d, p. 104). The continuous attack on linking, attacking mental processing by splitting, is so intense that Bion spoke of fragmentation. He further conceptualised these attacks from the inside as the work of an obstructive internal object, a kind of murderous superego that is the opposite of a containing object, or good internal breast.

These insights proved to be extremely valuable in working with psychotic patients, in whom we witness the immense aggression that lies underneath this kind of destruction and self–attack. This was not theorised by Freud's conceptualisation of psychosis in terms of libido decathexis. Clinically, there is more destructive and dynamic power in a psychosis than a silent withdrawal of libido would suggest. The onset of psychosis has such a devastating impact on mental functioning that it may be compared with a nuclear disaster. Once I saw a patient who literally blinded himself due to psychotic guilt feelings because of masturbation.

Comparing Bion's ideas on psychosis in "Attacks on linking" with some of his later views

Although overwhelmingly new and far-reaching, the text under discussion dates from the very beginning of Bion's theoretical corpus. When we view the sessions referred to in "Attacks on linking" from the perspective of some of Bion's later insights as expressed some years later in "A theory of thinking" (1967e) and then further developed in the four books which he called the Seven Servants (Bion, 1984a,b,c, 1986), we can see that the stammer, the disjointed remarks, the sitting upright as part of a reaction that suggested the patient felt as though he had received a blow, and the convulsive movements correspond to what Bion later called beta-elements. They are at the level of evacuation that corresponds to the A6 category in his Grid. However, the clinical material of these psychotic patients reveals that many of the elements that Bion relates to psychosis correspond to a category other than evacuated beta-elements. There are also elements in the clinical case material of the psychotic patient that can be categorised as alpha-elements, in which, by definition, something barely psychic is present. "Feeling wet" and its analysis by the patient and by Bion is an example of such an alpha-element. The "blue haze" is another example of an alpha-element (B category in the Grid). It might be a kind of negative hallucination, something that remains as debris after the attack, but it undoubtedly has a psychic quality. The probability clouds are images (C category in the Grid) with a psychic quality that remains after the attack on linking.

In his hypothesis about the underlying mechanism of the attacks on linking, Bion made a link with the Kleinian theory of attacks on the breast and the creative couple. In "Attacks on linking" he uses Kleinian preconceptions such as urinary attacks, mental urine. We may wonder whether the later Bion as we know him from his clinical seminars (Bion, 1987) would have seen this as reductive. But even starting from this classical background, he introduces something new in "Attacks on linking": invisible visual hallucinations that result from attacks by splitting up and fragmenting is an interesting concept. Bion will develop this further in *Transformations* (1984c) with his idea of a greedy, empty point that is annihilating, denuding everything of any sense.

The problem posed by $\leftarrow\uparrow$[1] can be stated by analogy with *existing* objects. $\leftarrow\uparrow$ is violent, greedy, and envious, ruthless, murderous, and predatory, without respect for the truth, persons, or things. It is, as it were, what Pirandello might have called a Character in Search of an Author. In so far as it has found a "character", it appears to be a completely immoral conscience. "This force is dominated by an envious determination to possess everything that objects that exist possess, including existence itself" (Bion, 1984c, p. 102).

Bion's technique

The clinical material in "Attacks on linking" also makes it possible to consider Bion's technique at the time it was written. As we discussed, he then related psychosis to inborn hate and aggression and to a malfunctioning of projective identification as communication, because the carer did not function as a good container. This could be because the contained is too strong and/or the container is not able to function properly. We might wonder whether Bion was a good container for the evacuated parts of the patient during the sessions. From the material, it is difficult to evaluate to what degree he was taking them in and digesting them, so that they could be given back to the patient in a metabolised way that would allow him to use them as building blocks for his mental functioning. That is the way we would see it nowadays. What Bion describes as containment makes us think of his motto: *fluc-*

tuat nec mergitur, which is also the motto of the city of Paris. He is rocked but not drowned by the material of the patient. He carries on being an analyst in the patient's strange world, by analysing and giving interpretations. He seems to be functioning more like a good soldier who keeps calm and carries on than providing the kind of mother function that we tend to associate "containment" with nowadays, even when we know that it is originally a military term.

The relationship between the obstructive object and omnipotent phantasy and the difference between a sane and an insane psychotic

An interesting idea of Bion's, which finds expression in "Attacks on linking", is that, to Bion, projective identification is not just at the level of phantasy; something is really passing over from the patient to the analyst. The descriptions in the text of "feeling wet" linked with the phantasy of being powerful, the falling piece of iron, and the anxiety of being murdered are examples of this. They can be understood as intended to evoke a feeling in the analyst. Furthermore, there seems to be a link with an underlying omnipotent phantasy. This omnipotent phantasy makes the patient behave in a way that is characterised by curiosity (trying to get in, to make contact by projective identification), arrogance (deriving from the omnipotent phantasy), and stupidity (due to the rigidity and lack of reality testing of the omnipotent phantasy). When these three characteristics are present, psychosis is lurking, according to Bion (1967c) in his paper "On arrogance". Bion does not make the link explicitly, but we can suppose that there is a link between such omnipotent phantasies and the obstructive object, as both are rooted in the same origin. The obstructive object as I described it above in this text is a kind of cruel, primitive superego which is linked with the primal disaster. The omnipotent phantasy is a defence against the attacks of the obstructive object. Drawing on the ideas that Bion (1986) elaborates in *Attention and Interpretation*, we might wonder whether the link between the obstructive object and the omnipotent phantasy is parasitic, commensal, or symbiotic? It seems symbiotic in the sense that the obstructive object and the primitive superego reinforce each other at the expense of the ego. The relationship between the obstructive object and the omnipotent phantasy seems to be the core dilemma (Badaracco & Vermote, 2002), the eye of the needle in the treatment of psychotic people. When the obstructive object retreats and the omnipotent phantasy is dissolved, only debris is left. The patient feels annihilated, as though he no longer exists. He is confronted with the fact that he was crazy. The anxiety that accompanies this realisation and the idea that it is caused by thinking might result in further evacuative projection and a new psychotic breakdown. It is a matter of life and death. Regarding the relationship between the obstructive object and the omnipotent phantasy, Bion (1967f) made an interesting distinction between a sane and an insane psychotic. An insane psychotic is someone who cannot tolerate the infinity of the unknown and clings to his omnipotent phantasy, while a sane psychotic (as Bion considered himself to be) can tolerate the infinity. The emptiness resulting from the crumbling of the omnipotent phantasy can be a blessing for the sane psychotic and the mystic but not for the insane psychotic, whose life is then felt to be worthless. The choice between holding to the omnipotent phantasy and remaining sick on the one hand and losing everything and regaining health on the other hand, is crucial.

Two clinical examples where obstructive object–omnipotent phantasy and a closing attitude towards the unknown go hand in hand

John is a patient who became psychotic while he was at university, when a girl did not respond to his advances. He experienced this as a kind of gap, maybe, rather, an abyss or a maelstrom that he covered with a delusion. During the onset of his acute psychosis, his mother was presented as a cruel witch (the obstructive object). He was completely confused and hallucinated. Gradually, his rational thinking recovered and he was even able to graduate, but his psychosis remained in a corner of his mind, to use Freud's expression. He was covering the gap with an omnipotent phantasy which he knew was a bit eerie, but nevertheless felt was true. He thought that he was a genius, and that the university was holding him back because he was too smart. He was sure that the dean of his faculty had intervened to convince the girl he was attracted to that she should leave him alone. With dazzling insight, he once compared himself to an albatross—

clumsy on the sand, but full of grace when flying in the air. On the basis of these ideas, he constructed a delusional system based on watertight logic. Only the starting point was false and psychotic. From that point on, it was as though the world was reduced to this one sterile, delusional story, that he told every session in the same tone. Often, when he thought he was unobserved by others, he would talk to himself, murmuring bizarre things and often shouting when alone on the street. I understood this as an evacuation of tension. The telling of the same story went on and on, and once, when I tried to interrupt and to blow some life into the system, he blocked me, stating that psychotherapy is free association and that I had to listen and keep my mouth shut.

In one particular session, it struck me that the patient was telling the same story but less monotonously and that he seemed rather agitated. When I learned what had happened, it turned out that he had applied for a job, but, because he was behaving strangely, he was not accepted. He did not mention this during our session, but I could feel that there was something. Retelling the same story every time was like a defensive blanket that prevented me from having contact with him, and prevented him from having contact with himself. That day, however, although the blanket was the same, it was disarranged by the underlying emotions that he denied. He needed his blanket, especially after this frustrating experience.

Peter is a university student who never showed any overt psychotic symptoms. The strange thing is that while he did not pass his exams at the university, he holds the university and psychiatric services responsible for this. They destroyed his future and he is convinced that the university should pay him back for his lost time, his treatment, and should make an exception to allow him to finish his studies in half of the time. The omnipotent idea is that he can do this, of course. It is frightening that he thinks he will commit suicide if he is not allowed to do this, which is almost certain. His thinking has become so closed that there is no space at all for alternatives. There is no hint of any capacity to be open to the unknown. When he gained financial means, his thinking became even more closed. His few social contacts are peers who believe his story and admire him for his intelligence. He never goes home and lives outside society. His life has become debris, in Bion's terms. There is no longer any way out. In this case, too, the omnipotent phantasy and the obstructive object that strips everything of any meaning go hand in hand. In my work with him, my endeavour is to open up his world, to allow him to accept something of the unknown. But the pain of relinquishing his omnipotent phantasy and seeing where he really is at this moment is unbearable.

Looking at the clinical material of "Attacks on linking" in the light of Bion's later approach: staying as close to the infinite as possible

The idea of clinging to an omnipotent phantasy can be linked with Bion's vision in later texts that a psychotic feels lost in an enormous space. Bion compared this experience with the opening of all the veins in a body at once, so that there is no longer enough blood to fill them, which results in a surgical shock. Bion (1986) even insisted that human beings invented geometry not because it reflects reality, but as a framework to protect themselves from getting lost in these infinite spaces. We could hear the clinical material in the paper in this sense: a haze, an invisible hallucination, probability clouds giving an impression that there is nothing to hold on to. This is in contrast with a transformation in O, where losing oneself in awe of the infinite unknown can have a liberating and changing effect. For the psychotic, getting lost involves a dissolution without any possibility of recovery (Bion refers to Pascal: *ces espaces infinies m'effrayent* (1984c, p. 171)) and therefore (insane) psychotics cling anxiously to a rigid delusional phantasy, thereby closing mentally and sticking to a sterile, often logically constructed, delusional thought.

We can consider Bion's work as consisting of mainly two parts (Vermote, 2011): the earlier part that is focused on transformations in K (thinking, making experiences psychic) up to the end of his book *Transformations* (1984c), and the later part on transformations in O (allowing new transforming experiences to happen, stemming from a world outside verbal thinking). In these two parts, Bion's attitude towards psychosis differs. In the T(K) part there is not such a great difference between the state of mind of the analyst (the paranoid–schizoid position) and of the psychotic; both have to try from a paranoid–schizoid state of mind to make what is not psychic become psychic. From T(O), however, there is a major difference between the analyst and the psychotic patient. While the analyst must be as open as possible to the undifferentiated, infinite, a-sensuous experience of non-verbal thinking, the psychotic closes himself off from this world in his insane psychosis.

In returning to the paper under discussion, and looking at Bion's attitude, we see that he is trying to understand the patient, whereas, in his later work, he will see rational understanding as a hindrance to seeing or intuiting constant conjunctions and patterns. He is thinking at a sensuous level, wanting to help and relieve anxiety; this kind of thinking is based on the pleasure principle. Later, he will state that in order to see patterns in the material of the psychotic patient, the analyst must be as close as possible to an infinite, a-sensuous level and see intuitively how something evolves and takes form from there. As readers, we cannot achieve this with Bion's paper, as we are too far from what happens in the session to allow this process to happen in ourselves. Bion (1967f) makes this criticism in his "Commentary" on his own text: why is it so difficult to communicate something of the experience of the session, so that we can think and rethink the material, so that it may be open to the future rather than being an argument in support of a theoretical insight. Indeed, as readers, we should be able to associate to the clinical material. We can try to do it ourselves using the few materials that we have, such as the blue haze evoking Jimmy Hendrix's purple haze, the probability clouds suggesting the horrible and fascinating mushroom cloud and destruction of the atomic bomb, time standing still, as in the Nagasaki museum, time frozen on melted watches, as in Dali's work. Space and time expand; there is nothing to hold on to. But our contact with the original material is too sparse for this exercise to be satisfactory.

Later, Bion (1986) describes how, in an analysis with a psychotic patient, the image of a monomolecular plane allowed him to visualise the contact that he had with his patient (perhaps this was the same patient as in the "Attacks on linking" paper). He gives this as an example of the importance of being in an a-sensuous state (without memory, desire, and understanding) to listen to psychotic patients. It might seem counter-intuitive to maintain this analytic attitude with psychotics; one might expect that it would be preferable to maintain as much contact with reality as possible, in order to avoid losing one's grip and making them more crazy. However, Bion insists that, for psychotics, this analytic stance without memory, desire, and understanding is important.

Since his realisation of the "monomolecular plane image", he understood the patient much better, although he was not sure that it helped the patient, as the transformation had taken place in him and not in the patient (Bion, 1986).

As far as I understand it, Bion (1986) proposed to see beta, alpha, C, and the other categories of the Grid as separate vectors in space, each following its own line, which might meet or not. They can express the same thing, but becoming conscious or understood depends on their meeting. In this psychic functioning, a sense of infinity is manifest. This is a different perspective from understanding the categories or elements as being transformed from the one into the other by mental processing or thinking, as Bion had in most of his work so far. The beta level vectors include the stammer, sitting upright, anxiety, being overwhelmed; the C vector is indicated by poetic phrases such as blue haze and probability clouds. We can also discern other vectors coming from the unknown, infinite zone. There are infinite possibilities. They are probes into the unknown, to use Bion's words. We can link these vectors in our mind as analysts, but this does not mean that they are linked in the mind of the patient. We must blind ourselves, says Bion (1986) (following Freud, in his letter to Lou Andreas Salomé) in order to intuit links at an a-sensuous level. Then we are more in contact with the patient and able to tolerate his fragmented state, rather than filling it up with our own narratives. Then we are more open to the few links that the patient might make. Bion compares this with directing a beam of intense darkness.

The late Bion suggests that the analyst should be radically open to the vast unknown that the psychotic is confronted with, having no reference points to hold on to. This unknown space is so vast that it leads to stammering and shock. Is the stammer a defective way of speaking, or a language that points to the patient's inner world? As in Isaiah 33:19, "Thou shalt not see a fierce people, a people of a deeper speech than thou canst perceive; of a stammering tongue, that thou canst not understand".

Can the vector of stammer and shock be coupled with that of the poetic blue haze and probability clouds? Can they marry, so to speak, and can the patient become a sane psychotic this way, and speak from an "awe for the unknown" without being entrapped in the sterile, unchangeable, delusional system? Is an evolution leading from insane to sane psychosis possible? Bion's later ideas seem to go in this direction.

A personal interpretation on the phenomenon of attacks on linking, based on Bion's work

In my view, in Bion's work we see an evolution to a model of different layers in psychic functioning. Three major layers are Reason, with thinking based on verbal thought and finite, Transformations in Knowledge that result from an automatic, creative, ongoing psychic processing which happens mostly at an unconscious level, a kind of "waking dream thought" which happens, so to speak, at a mixed undifferentiated–differentiated level, as we also see in dreams (Matte Blanco, 1988), and transformations in O, which are related to a psychic functioning at a level of non-verbal, direct, intuitive experience and are, therefore, infinite. This model can also be related to neuroscientific findings about psychic functioning (Vermote, 2014).

In the light of this model, the phenomenon of "attacks on linking" can be seen, at the level of transformation in knowledge, as attacking the stream of waking dream thought or unconscious, creative, automatic linking. Bion supposes the patient then has to make links at the level of Reason, which results in links that are logical, but sterile and dead as far as emotions are concerned.

However, in order to allow transformations in O, which are concerned with direct intuitive contact, to take place, such attacks on linking of pre-existing thoughts are fundamental. Bion's adage, no memory, no desire, no coherence, no understanding can be understood as a thorough attack on linking. With this attitude of total openness to experience, which Bion calls Faith, there is a paradoxically enhanced functioning of the internal, creative, automatic thinker that is at work at the middle layer of Transformations in Knowledge.

Conclusion

Bion's ideas on attacks on linking had a great impact on the understanding of psychosis and borderline pathology. This is later elaborated in his theory of thinking with alpha and beta elements. In the light of his theory of transformations, these early theories are about Transformation in Knowledge and how this is attacked. Trying to enhance this kind of transformation is a problem that the psychoanalyst and the psychotic patient share. The perspective of transformations in O allows another approach to the problem of psychosis. From this point of view, when a psychotic patient closes himself to the a-sensuous, infinite, undifferentiated reality that is O, he is seen as an insane psychotic. When he can be open to it, he becomes a sane psychotic. The relationship with O now becomes the most important difference for psychosis.

Note

1. A movement in the Grid that represents attacks on linking and stripping of meaning, unlike that which Bion formulated as "negative growth".

References

Badaracco, J. G., & Vermote, R. (2002). The nature of the problems of psychoanalysis with so-called 'difficult' patients. *International Journal of Psychoanalysis, 83*: 689–694.

Bion, W. R. (1967a). *Second Thoughts: Selected Papers on Psychoanalysis*. New York: Jason Aronson.

Bion, W. R. (1967b). The imaginary twin. In: *Second Thoughts* (pp. 3–22). New York: Jason Aronson.

Bion, W. R. (1967c). On arrogance. In: *Second Thoughts* (pp. 86–92). New York: Jason Aronson.

Bion, W. R. (1967d). Attacks on linking. In: *Second Thoughts* (pp. 93–109). New York: Jason Aronson.

Bion, W. R. (1967e). A theory of thinking. In: *Second Thoughts* (pp. 110–119). New York: Jason Aronson.

Bion, W. R. (1967f). Commentary. In: *Second Thoughts* (pp. 120–166). New York: Jason Aronson.

Bion, W. R. (1984a). *Learning from Experience*. London: Karnac.

Bion, W. R. (1984b). *Elements of Psychoanalysis*. London: Karnac.

Bion, W. R. (1984c). *Transformations*. London: Karnac.

Bion, W. R. (1986). *Attention and Interpretation*. London: Karnac.

Bion, W. R. (1987). *Clinical Seminars and Other Works*, F. Bion (Ed.). London: Karnac.

Matte Blanco, I. (1988). *Thinking, Feeling and Being: Clinical Reflections on the Fundamental Antinomy of Human Beings*. London: Routledge.

Vermote, R. (2011). On the value of 'Late Bion' to analytic theory and practice. *International Journal of Psychoanalysis, 92*: 1089–1098.

Vermote, R. (2014). Transformations et transmissions du fonctionnement psychique—approche integrative et implications cliniques. *Revue française de psychanalyse, LXXVIII*: 389–405.

CHAPTER FIVE

"Attacks on linking": the transformation of emotional experiences and its obstacles

Elizabeth Lima da Rocha Barros and
Elias Mallet da Rocha Barros

What is the connection between being depressed about a haircut that went wrong, angry divergences over inflation rates, the criteria for choosing boyfriends/a future husband, and rivalry? Apparently, there is none, at least not in the conscious sphere of the patient we will discuss below, when she reported clinical material associated with these topics. From her perspective, these accounts are expressions of conscious perceptions and opinions regarding the analyst's behaviour, and her own private and social life. We suggest that, at the level of the unconscious mental dynamics, these views originate from forms of relating with the world that are manifestations expressive of the nature of the existing relationships between internal objects. The initially concrete character of the verbal manifestations and their apparent disconnection during the session commented on later in the chapter result, in our view, from projective identifications and splits that restrict her capacity for symbolic expression. We begin with the patient's dream and then use this material to reflect on the dream's unconscious meanings and their relation to the potential attacks on linking that these reveal.

This dream happened after a session in which the patient—whom we will call Lucia—said that she had refused to make an executive decision in her work due to her ethical principles. She was indignant over a colleague's proposal, considering it to be at the bounds of ethics, though legally defensible. Her indignation was associated, according to Lucia, to a matter the analyst (first author) and the patient had been discussing. The analyst had proposed a raise in fees and the patient had reacted strongly against this, also in the name of ethics, as in her work. The patient argued that, inflation being very low in Brazil at the time of the session, no raise could be justified beyond a simple readjustment in accordance with the inflation rate reflecting this. Increases in gross value would be immoral within the present economic situation, she thought. She emphasised that her questioning was not due to any financial difficulty of her own, but arose solely from her moral perspective.

In the session that we will now report, in which the dream comes up, the patient walks in and says she hesitated a lot before coming. She was to give a seminar lecture to investors after the session, and needed to look good for this. She was afraid that the session might upset her, and she would end up "looking bad". Then, indignant, she comments that it was enough for her that day what her hairdresser had done to her hair. She had been stupid in agreeing with the proposal of a change in haircut, which ended up horrible. Many months would be needed for her to recover the original style, she says angrily.

We would like here to pinpoint her revolt and anger clearly expressed regarding the damage to her image resulting from a haircut she had not approved of, as she put it, but had been seduced into accepting.

At this point in the session, she remembers a dream.

The dream

> She was checking her bank balance in a Swiss bank when, to her surprise, she discovered she had two accounts. In the second, she had a partner (joint account), the colleague of the unethical proposal. Large amounts were deposited in this second account, originating from not quite honest procedures. For an instant, she thought of transferring the revenues from this joint account to her other private and legal account, attracted by the financial tranquillity and security such a balance would afford her. And, after all, both accounts were hers, and she had held them for long time, for more than ten years.

On leaving the bank, she was met by a driver and two *seguranças* (bodyguards; in Portuguese, the term for bodyguard is *segurança,* or security man. *Segurança* is also the word for self-security), who worked for a known *doleiro* (Black Market agent for buying and selling dollars outside the official Central Bank rates), a swindler. She found it odd, but, as she was leaving a bank, she thought it good to have these *seguranças* to protect her, though at the same time feeling a bit disturbed, trying to understand how this had come about.

Next, she is submitting herself to a magnetic resonance imaging (MRI) scan. The doctor assisting her is fat, very pleasant, and she feels strongly attracted to him. [He reminds Lucia of the fiancé she broke up with to marry her present husband, with whom she has had many matrimonial hardships, a possible divorce being contemplated at the present moment. This fiancé was a childhood friend, very loving, pleasant, a fine talker (a *causeur*), and she felt well understood by him. However, he was very ugly and offered no financial security. Her present husband appeared at that time in her life, that is, when she was engaged to the first boyfriend. Within three months of being together with the new, handsome fiancé, she decided to get married to him. He was very good-looking and rich, in contrast to her former fiancé. Her relationship with her husband has been a disaster. To think about what to do and arrive at a decision regarding this had been the theme of several difficult sessions lately.]

Returning to the dream, she relates that after feeling attracted to the doctor,

> she panicked, as she remembered that she was pregnant and thought that the magnetic resonance would harm her baby. On leaving the MRI room, she looked at herself in the mirror to check if her pregnancy was visible. She couldn't understand how she could have forgotten her pregnancy and also asked herself, indignant, if the doctor hadn't noticed. The problem at stake was to figure out whose responsibility it was for her entering an MRI scan at so improper a time. She did not like what she saw in the mirror on leaving. She felt ugly and saw also the fat doctor reflected, who, next to her, no longer seemed so pleasant and disquieted her, especially being so close to her when she already felt ugly due to her pregnant belly, she added. She remarked, still in the dream: *And on top of it, with this fat man beside me!*

There was another important detail in the dream. The MRI scan cost more than a painting she had sold recently and for this reason also she felt indignant.

Actually, she says, commenting on the dream, none of what is there mentioned was related to reality and the financial sums in the bank accounts were absurd. She had no account in Switzerland and had never thought of having one, although professionally she dealt with deposits in foreign banks, including the Swiss banks. Neither had she recently sold any work of art.

Some considerations

The Greeks did not say one has had a dream, but one has seen a dream (Dodds, 1965, p. 17). The fact of the dream presenting itself through images seems central in considering the nature of this psychic work and will reveal itself to be very important to our considering how links are established between emotional experiences and the functions carried out by internal objects. Freud spoke of dream-work as a mental activity carried out on psychic material so as to promote what he called migration towards figurability; from this movement ensues its predominantly visual form.

We must add that the language of evocation is inherent to visual images that prevail in dreams and result from dream-work that compresses experiences into images. These images are deeply influenced by forms of relations with internal objects in the inner world (da Rocha Barros, E., 1997). Thanks to these characteristics, dreams constitute the freest form of association between emotional experiences, as they are stored in the unconscious mind and provide us access to how individuals organise and give meaning intrapsychically to their intersubjective emotional (affective) experiences.

Figurability also allows for various independent or disconnected facts to be represented in a single scene. We believe that in the dreamt scenes are represented compacted emotional experiences originating in diverse areas and different times in the life of this patient. These links, however, are not present in Lucia's mind consciously, so that she might have used them to have a more global vision of the meanings underlying her states of mind and what she said in the session. As such, her capacity to reflect on how her emotions are sparked off by situations taking place in the present in her personal relations is restricted. Without the presence of these connections, the patient relates with her external world more by projective identifications than through reflexive responses regarding an objective situation.

Stokes (1972) refers to forms as being one to the eye but multiple to the mind, or, better, containing multiple meanings due to various generated evocations.

Ferro (1995) refers also to this compacting of experiences present in dream images saying they are "the syncretic naming of emotions [in this case in the form of images] in search of (not necessarily anthropomorphic) characters that will make narrative developments possible" (p. 109, translated for this edition). In another paper (Rocha Barros, E. M., 2000), we suggested that these images are affective pictograms. A pictogram is, therefore, neither a choice nor free creation, but the result of the laws that govern the activity of representation (Aulagnier, 1986. See especially Chapter IV).

Ferro (1995) describes the "dreamlike photogram of the waking state," which acts as an affective hologram of the analytic pair and can be regarded as a syncretic designation of emotions. Bion (1992, p. 52), too, used the term ideogram to refer to an analogical figuration that records mental phenomena for storage in the mind. We use pictogram in a related way, to refer to a very early form of mental representation of emotional experiences, fruit of the alpha function, that creates symbols by means of figurations for dream-thought, as the foundation for, and first step toward, thought processes. Strictly speaking, however, pictograms are not yet thought processes, since they are expressed in images and contain powerful expressive–evocative elements rather than in verbal discourse.

The statement that dream images are part of a process of transforming experiences so as to allow them thinkability (Ferro, 1999, p. 82), represents an important change to Freud's theory of dreams.

What we wish to underline is that dream images emanate from configurations of internal object relations and we are using for them the term "kernels of meaning" of emotional life that have a structuring function of the psyche. These kernels act from the unconscious, as mental structures attributing meaning to our emotional experiences.

Authors from diverse theoretical orientations differing from Freud attribute today an integrating function to dreams (which, at times, fails) making for greater cohesiveness of the ego. Palombo (1978), for example, speaks of the integration of new perceptions to established structures, and Stolorow and Atwood (1993) refer to dream activity as part of a process of preserving and/or facilitating structures necessary for development. Klein (1975), on introducing in her model of the psychic apparatus the notion of an internal world, indicates by implication another status and a new function to dreams in mental life. These become, in this new context, sources of knowledge about the inner theatre of meanings, and the action present in the dream is expressive, we suggest, of specific configurations of relations between internal objects. We wish to underscore that it is through dreams that our previous emotional experiences, stimulated by our current emotional experiences, are transformed and, thus, worked through, or metabolised. For us, this is the central function of dreaming and, therefore, a central standpoint in this chapter.

In this context, the dream ceases being merely a scene put on a stage on which conflicts find expression, that is, a compromise formation in order to allow the dreamer to continue sleeping, and becomes something much more complex. The oneiric space transforms itself into the very stage where the mind tries to solve these conflicts, affording them a first form towards thinkability. In this context, Meyer (2014) writes,

> I believe the dream is an expressive means by which the psychic apparatus delineates, builds, and communicates an issue being confronted. The key word here is "issue". Put another way: for the dream to exist a problem must be identified, gain shape, and be conveyed to an other. These operations, in their turn, allow us to see, through transparency, the mode of functioning and the structure of the psychic apparatus that generated them, for there it has its origin. For example, that which is "chosen" by the dreamer as an issue informs us about the perceptive focus of the psychic structure; in its turn, the resulting expressive form tells us about the resources that exist to produce it. (Translated for this edition)

It follows that if we adopt the perspective that the dream also has the function of integrating the ego and of transforming emotional experiences through the creation or re-establishment of links in a process of enlarging the mental field, then we must attribute to dreams a function other than that of merely disguising unconscious infantile wishes to allow sleep to continue.

For Freud, it was the repressed infantile desires, associated with present experiences, which were the triggering element of dreams. For him, the links that were split were those connecting conscious feelings with the unconscious repressed infantile life and, therefore, the past infancy with adult life.

In the approach now adopted, we are suggesting that links are attacked and cut off in the unconscious when their connection produces unbearable psychic suffering and, in consequence, it is the metabolising or digestive capacity of the mind that is affected.

The world of dreams from this stance harbours a continuous process of transformation of emotional experiences in which our inner dramas are processed. To understand this continuous process of working through, Bion offers us as instruments the theory of the alpha function, the dialectical relation between positions, the model of the relation container–contained, and the theory of emotional links (L, H, K). Transformations can be understood within the interactive model proposed by these elements.

What would the patient have *seen* by means of the images of this dream and, we should perhaps add, what would she have *obscured and, therefore, hidden* by means of these same images? Or, in other words, what links would be potentially present in these images and/or which would be blocked as the outcome of an attack? And what would be the nature of this attack?

Bion (1967) refers to the attacks on linking that the patient makes on anything which is "felt to have the function of linking one object with another" (p. 93, item 92). Later on, Bion (1967) justifies the use of the word link, stating,

> I employ the term "link" because I wish to discuss the patient's relationship with a function rather than with the object that subserves a function; my concern is not only with the breast, or penis or verbal thought, but with their function of providing the link between two objects. (p. 102, item 96)

Examining the dream

Let us now see whether these processes of attacks on linking and their consequences can be identified in operation during this session and also try to clarify their function. In a first approach, when considering the conscious material of the patient, we could say that we are observing the consequences of these attacks on linking. These attacks are presented through a state of irritation, opposition, and ill will regarding the analyst, in the wish not to come to the session and in a state of mind of a slightly paranoid connotation tainted by a generalised discomfort. In the session, the world represented by the analyst is experienced as hostile and threatening.

Only after understanding and interpreting analytically these consequences can we mobilise the emotional experiences that amplify the affective network and create or re-establish unconscious links needed for allowing the process of working through to take place. The related dream affords the occasion to widen our understanding of what is happening unconsciously in the internal world of this patient.

Let us now look back at the session in detail. It begins with the patient worried over the impact of her appearance on others and with the damage that the analyst might cause were she to insist on trying to understand her, for she did not want to look bad while lecturing to a group of investors at her bank.

The hairdresser had already "damaged" her, and she "had been an idiot" for accepting his promise that his intervention would improve her appearance, she believes.

Here, we find out that she is a person focused on whatever might improve or damage her appearance, but that she does not believe that any attempt at improving her mind/head will lead to anything good or advantageous to her. The analyst is associated with the hairdresser, as she also deals with her head/mind and, implicitly, has an effect on her appearance.

We can see in this expressive account of an emotional experience undergone in the session how the absence of links contributes to the *belief* that her inner and outer objects are only capable of promoting a deterioration of her image. At this point, it is interesting to note that Britton (1998) reminds us that *believing is a form of object relating*. This expectation of incapacity to understand her on the analyst's part representing her internal objects, keeps her from having a more peaceful state of mind.

For reasons yet unknown to the patient, these ideas result in an association with the dream related right after. This one, for its content, seems associated with the previous session and the recollection of the proposal by her work partner that had sparked indignation.

Oddly, however, the patient in the dream is in a Swiss bank, being the holder of two accounts, of which she asserts she had no previous knowledge, it being that one of them is a secret account where illicit deposits are made, but the other is lawful and legal from the standpoint of Brazilian law. When she leaves the bank she feels protected, in this situation, by two *seguranças* (bodyguards) who, in the external world are associated with giving protection to an actually existing known swindler. Switzerland is the country of secret accounts, a secure place for illicit investments.

What would these two accounts represent? What might be illicit about one of them, according to her inner perception?

We know that she behaves, in real life, as a paladin of honesty. In the dream, however, she is clearly involved in illicit activities, from which she gets benefits. How to understand this dream in relation with the analyst? What are the transferential elements present? She begins the session apprehensive about one more time being victim to indecent proposals, for example, letting herself be interpreted by the analyst, or, better, letting herself be deluded by her into believing that, through a deeper psychoanalytic examination and understanding of her feelings, she could improve her appearance and, as a result of this positive experience, come to accept a raise in fees, among other things.

Following Bion, we should ask what functions of the analyst as internal object are being attacked? We are suggesting that as a result of these attacks, some emotions are suppressed in favour of others, in this case more hostile ones, triggering a sort of despair that hinders a more objective contact with the reality of facts.

Going back to the dream, next we have a change in scene. She is no longer in the bank, but in a doctor's office. In this oneiric space, she is also involved in an issue of values (financial) that are questionable: the scan costs more than a painting she sold recently. (Consciously, she knows this did not happen, and neither is it true.) Again, a reference to competing values that is the cost of medical consultations, which is related to the analyst's raise in fees that likely arouses in her competitive feelings, but there are other elements. She is attracted to the doctor, who, nevertheless, is fat and ugly. That leads her to recalling, spontaneously, her fiancé whom she left to get married, within only three months, to her present husband because he was good looking and rich.

Suddenly, still in the dream, Lucia goes into a panic. She is pregnant, and the medical examination might harm her. Once again the worry over appearance is present, when she gets up to look in the mirror to see if her pregnancy shows. There is another worry, subsidiary to this one. Would it be her responsibility not to have mentioned the pregnancy, or the doctor's? She sees herself as ugly in the mirror, the attractive doctor loses his charm, becoming unpleasant, as he contributes to reflecting an image of hers that is rather unattractive now.

The reader can grasp the emotions involved in this sequence and, as such, conjecture as to how the lack of awareness of certain links contributes to the patient's having a distorted view of reality which, in its turn, interferes with her capacity to make choices in her best interest. This distorted and defensive perception, however, protects her from the psychic pain which she would probably suffer were she aware of how she made these choices governed by her narcissism and desire for power, reflected in the image of a rich and handsome husband.

Discussion

The interpretation of the dream aims to reveal the process of meaning building in the internal world of the patient. For psychic change to occur, it is necessary that the analyst help to identify the kernels of unconscious meaning underneath the emotional experiences involved so that these can be put in the form of verbal symbols proper to be thought. These, in their turn, enable the creation and/or reestablishment of links between emotional experiences that before either did not exist or were attacked in such a way as to prevent the patient from facing any psychic suffering.

We believe, in the case of this patient, that the action in the dream begins to take shape in the previous session, when she becomes competitively indignant over the analyst's proposal to raise the fees. The patient's worth, her self-image, according to her feeling, is put competitively under question simply by her going to the analyst asking for help and understanding. In a next moment in the session, the patient begins fearing being confronted with her own real unconscious reasons for avoiding such a psychoanalytic examination, since the result of this revelation might damage her self-image as a paragon of ethical correctness.

We think that Lucia has some awareness of her competitiveness but not the least—and would never gain deeper access without the help of an analyst—as to the network of meanings opened by this competitiveness. Above all, we believe that she does not have access to all that she is willing to give up for this competitiveness in preserving and polishing up her external appearance. Her indignation at the analyst's proposal seems founded on sources less noble than she would like consciously. The threat to her image sparked by the proposal connects with the conflicts with which she is being confronted in having to examine the unconscious nature of her relationship with her husband, in the present, in her dissatisfaction with her marriage.

In this context is formed, as we see it, the action of the dream. It is shaped from that which we are calling kernels of meaning. The kernel here refers to her competitive unconscious investment in her appearance working against her more intimate feelings about what better answers her needs.

In the process of apprehending the kernels of meaning operating in the unconscious as poles of attraction, there is already an attempt at working through the conflicts by constituting an internal space where meaning is built and which generates forms of symbolic representation.

We suggest that this attempt at working through the conflict appears in the dream in the form of an incipient awareness, transmuted and expressed in plastic figurations, of an asked question. The issue in this case is her doubt regarding the source of the values she has, represented by the two accounts in Switzerland, one legal and the other illicit. Those two accounts represent two different processes of growing up into maturity and integration, presented in the dream as a dilemma. The first is more genuine and is based on taking in food for thought. The second is based on taking over, through projective identification, of qualities and values that she envies in the other, represented by the analyst in the session.

In the internal theatre of the dream, Lucia is tempted to believe that if she takes on the values deposited in her second, secret, illicit account, she will gain security and peace. What illicit values would these be?

We suggest that the account considered legal is the one in which would be deposited the values associated with mature psychic growth, represented by an attitude of taking in, of accepting food for growth coming from an object that is a good provider of the capacity to think. The second account, the illicit one, is associated with an attitude of taking over another's values (money standing for qualities, too) to feed into her grandiosity. From this viewpoint, the attack would be directed at the link holding the function of nurturing the capacity to think carried out by the analyst through her observations/interpretations. To depend on the analyst as a source of enriching her capacity to think is experienced by her as a challenge to her narcissistic omnipotence.

On attacking the analyst in her nurturing function, the patient projects hostile feelings into this object, making it threatening and virtually incapable of understanding her.

We believe she projects aggressive feelings into the analyst and, in this way, transforms her into a sadistic superego who wishes to deprive Lucia of her good looks (physical appearance). A similar superegoic dynamic was recently discussed by O'Shaughnessy (2011) who characterided this type of superegoic functioning as being an extractor of worth and pointer at failure (p. 176). In the sessions we are describing, Lucia does not see any value in the analyst or in the doctor in the dream representing her long-lasting loving relationship with her first fiancé. The question is, now, how would this superego have developed? Our hypothesis is that it is the outcome of envious attacks on the primary maternal object, later internalised, identified with a mother who attacks her child, anticipating that she will disappoint her in her high narcissistic ideals.

We must consider, reflecting on this issue, which she underscored at the beginning of the session, that she did not want to leave the analysis upset by the analyst's observations/interpretations. Also, in the dream, a deep examination of her body (through the MRI scan) is seen as harmful and provokes panic. This panic in the dream ensues from the image obtained in the scan. What would be the unconscious meaning of this fear represented in the dream by panic arising from the deep examination of her pregnancy through the MRI scan? The scan, from our psychoanalytic point of view, would show a child developing in her and would, thus, confront her with a psychic truth threatening her narcissism, in that she would be faced with the fact that the baby's growth does not happen automatically, but depends on being fed by the mother inside her body. If so, to grow it is necessary to depend on another person; in the session, to be dependent on the analyst. This dream, as we see it, is constituted from a dilemma present in her unconscious thought. To see the object implies valuing it, and, consequently, increasing unconsciously her feeling of dependence which would weaken her narcissistic perspective. Likewise, to accept paying more to the analyst would represent acknowledging her value to her.

Final considerations

Before concluding this chapter, we would like to address a more general but frequent question posed by some analysts: is it enough to dream in order to produce psychic change, as some analysts suggest, or is it absolutely necessary that an analyst interpret the dream, as others say? Has interpreting dreams fallen into disuse in contemporary psychoanalysis? How can these questions be seen in the light of the theory of attacks on links?

On this issue, we agree with Fédida (1996), who has suggested that the image of the dream isolated from interpretation is lost in a sort of autotelic knowledge: that is, which has its purpose limited and restricted just to the sole production of an image and nothing else. The images of the dream represent only part of the working through of ongoing emotional experiences, in as much as the psychic apparatus delineates, builds, and conveys an issue with which it is confronted (Meyer, 2014). However, we believe that some affective networks are not available for figurative representation in the mind.

It is necessary, therefore, that the analyst, through his interpretations, produces a transposition of the evocative language of the images to the verbal language that elucidates the meanings, as Meltzer (1984) states. In his words, "The dreamer enlists the aid of the analyst to transform the evocative descriptive language into the verbal language of the description of meaning, the first move towards abstraction and sophistication" (p. 52).

Let us take as an example Lucia's session in order to examine this issue in more detail. Can we believe that Lucia, just as a result of her dreaming and understanding some of the dream's contents, would promote changes leading her to a more integrated functioning? We would like to present some hypotheses concerning the limits of Lucia's understanding of her dream. There is no doubt that the dream is already part of a process of working through.

We understand that if she tried to analyse her dream, she would be blocked from most of her unconscious motives at stake in the session, shown in the form of her behaviour and discourse directed at her analyst. This is because the patient is cut off from knowing the real motives for which the analyst is attacked and nullified in her nourishing function. If she is so afraid of this examination (in the dream, of the MRI scan harming her), what would be the reason driving her into going deeper, on her own, into the meaning of the dream? But even if she wanted to go deeper, we still think there are unconscious dynamic elements resulting from attacks on linking which would block an examination of meanings in the dream beyond a certain point. Lucia would have access only to some interpretations, of an analogical sort, which would not account for the nature of the involved projective identifications. For example, she could suppose that the dream refers to how she felt the analyst, just like the colleague, was trying to gain dishonest advantages by proposing to raise the consultation fee above inflation rates. As such, the analyst appears as one who wants more money deposited in her account, a desire the patient took as an illicit form of relating with her. In wanting to be better paid, the analyst arouses envy in the patient, for Lucia feels herself diminished *vis-à-vis* the worth of the analyst. Perhaps, even, Lucia could think that she needs to be on the alert before accepting being examined.

We think these interpretations, which she could have reached on her own, would account only for some aspects of the dream, as they are directly associated with conscious opinions, due to dynamic elements which hinder her from a deeper examination of her own self. We think she has some elusive notion that a deeper psychoanalytic examining inside herself might be harmful, that is, painful, from what she could see. As such, we believe she would distance herself from her psychic reality, and would be deluded by her own interpretations, increasing her defences.

We are left with little doubt at this point as to the dream's being directly related with the previous session, with the proposed increase in fees which triggered her moralist (or righteous) attitude, that some dishonesty hovers around the scene of the session and the dream, the appearance issue is present in various forms, and that this is linked with dissatisfaction with the marriage, among other issues. It is not a matter of interpreting critically (super-egoic) the patient's mental functioning, but, rather, of examining the pillars of her present mental constitution, which leave her vulnerable before people or audiences (including those professionals) she will have to meet. Her ambivalence mentioned at the beginning of the session about coming or not to meet with the analyst results from the threat that a deep self-analytic examination might cause to her figure/appearance (she did not want to look bad, she says all the time). In a similar way, she projects these feelings on the audience which is to hear her after this session, believing it would be more focused on her appearance than on the content of her presentation.

We think that the obstacles to a deeper investigation of the dream by the patient are of two kinds: on the one hand, there are dynamic resistances against confronting psychic pain that a deep analytical examination would produce. On the other hand, we think also that there are factors associated with the nature of the imagetic/figurative language of the dreams that restrict access to knowledge that might be derived from it. This second factor will also affect the analyst.

There seems to be no doubt that the images present in the dream represent attempts at grasping certain feelings in the patient's inner world, giving them a plastic representation, a first form of thought. In this sense, the dream is part of the process of working through emotional experiences.

Now, we shall address some questions that arise in dealing with the difficulties encountered in examining the relations between images present in dreams (and in the mind) and their meanings. We shall continue to use Lucia's dream to discuss this issue.

The questions we are faced with are: do these images (or symbolic forms) already contain a meaning? Is it complete, or incipient? If it contains a meaning, can it be found by the patient herself, as I already mentioned, or is there need of help to do so?

We find that the meaning is not implicit in the images the dreamer sees in the dream, but that what is meaningful is outlined in the oneiric work of transformation of emotional contents that leads to building these images. On being built, these figurations are an attempt at representing an emotional reality apprehended in the internal world of the dreamer. For this reason, we believe that this dream asks for an intervention by the analyst, who is not subject to the same impeditive constraints as the patient.

So, what does the scene figured in Lucia's dream tell us? We would begin by considering it as a first symbolic form representing and expressing an internal dilemma. The patient wishes consciously to say meaningful and clear things about the present Brazilian economic situation and wants recognition, but, unconsciously, a narcissistic grandiosity related to her appearance threatens her confidence and capacity to develop her thoughts. In this narcissistic context, her audience becomes tainted by a malignant attitude towards her and more focused on her appearance than on her ideas.

In this scene, we believe the discursive elements are later additions evoked by the scene. We wish to emphasise that this scene—which also encompasses the relation between its constitutive components—represents and expresses through symbolic forms the nature of her anxiety, both in the session while relating to her analyst and also to the prospective audience for her talk. The condemnation or attribution of illegitimacy to the analyst's proposal of a raise in fees probably stems from a superegoic aspect made present at the moment that links to how she makes her romantic choices, which seems not to be present in her choice of a husband.

Melsohn (1989, p. 58) writes that the dream can be understood as a form of consciousness that presentifies (this word is a philosophical neologism) through images, emotional conceptions of the world. We would add that this consciousness is not evident on a first approach but exists virtually in the links that are likely to be established if emotional experiences are awakened in the intersubjective relation established with the analyst.

We think we can amplify this concept, suggesting that, besides presentifying, the dream reveals meaningful kernels of the emotional experiences which act as poles of attraction of meanings underlying our interpersonal relations and orientating them.

From this perspective the emotions (which, in themselves, are links) are not only symptomatic of states of mind, but, above all, represent, as we also mentioned, kernels of meaning of the experience. To become thinkable and communicable, emotions need to go through a transformation and acquire a symbolic form more suitable for this aim. As such, emotional situations also are transformed into symbolic forms—perhaps we could say affective pictograms (da Rocha Barros, 2000)—that function in mental life as attractive poles of meanings.

Evocative processes associated with emotional experiences are very powerful in shaping interpersonal behaviour. Evocative language is that which also prevails over projective identification processes. It is from evocative forms that each individual or patient draws his/her power to invite the other (in the session, the analyst) to enact certain roles independent of their will.

We think that the dream gives us access to these projective identifications, which express the world of object relations structured round unconscious phantasies. By being expressed through images of high evocative power, these processes are more accessible to the analyst through the dream.

It is not by chance that Resnik (1984) speaks of the world of dreams as a living forest in which dwells phantasy in a state of riddle (p. 17).

Unconscious phantasies, in their turn, are not merely accounts to be revealed in the session through a translation process seeking analogic equivalents in the speech of the patient. They are expressions of unconscious forms of thinking and shaping the world of relationships according to certain prevailing configurations in the internal world of the patient, organised around the kernels of meaning of the emotional experience. Some phantasies constitute themselves in beliefs and, as such, acquire a quality of an object relation. Britton (1998) writes regarding this,

> A belief is a phantasy invested with the qualities of a psychic object and believing is a form of object relating . . . I think belief is an act, it is in the realm of knowledge what attachment is in the realm of love. (pp. 12–13)

Every action in the dream represented by images takes place in the present and recalls another time and space, having a structuring function in psychic life with the same qualities as the Homeric poet, interpreter of *Mnenosyne,* who has the immediate experience of the past that happened, or we could say, is happening. In the oneiric space, to remember, know, see, are equivalent terms, and, thus, allow us contact with the immediate experience of the past.

From this conception ensues our stance of considering the patient's dream as carrying out a function similar to that of the theatre director who puts on stage and there narrates a personal scene of a psychic reality in the way it was built and transformed since childhood (Mancia, 1989).

We must also reflect upon the question of the conditions necessary for a dream to become the stage of the process of psychic working through. We think that the process of working through comprises various levels. It does not limit itself to apprehending an emotional experience *per se,* though this is its starting point. In order that the dream be part of a process of psychic working through, it is necessary to separate what is dream work from the observation of this process in the internal world of the patient. We find it meet to quote a passage of Meltzer's to enhance our discussion. He says,

> But if we are to allow that meaning goes beyond the perception of gestalten and that mental life goes beyond anything that one could imagine as a property of computers . . . [we would need to accept] the possibility that mentation is non-sensuous in its inception, that it is concerned with objects for whom forms need to be invented or borrowed from external reality, which has emotion as its central phenomenon and whose laws are not those of logic or mathematics, but of "progression" in formal qualities (S. Langer) or transformations (Bion). (Siqueira, 1991, p. 766, translated for this edition)

Now, a matter of psychoanalytic technique: what is the transferential connection of Lucia's dream and what is its possible interpretation?

We think the dream reflects her worry over letting herself be examined by the analyst, in the role of the doctor in the dream who understands her, but who challenges the pillars of her self-security based on questionable investments in her appearance, about which she is always concerned. The reference to the price of the magnetic resonance imaging in the dream, in comparison to the value of the painting she had sold, indicates her rivalry with the analyst, set off by the latter's asking for a raise in fees. The analyst, according to the patient's feelings, would be intending to be of more worth than she, in wanting to charge her more for a deeper psychoanalytic examination which, on the other hand, could damage her by its capacity to see deep inside her (her analytic MRI), putting in check the basis of her present self-security. The Swiss Bank which keeps her two accounts refers to the system in her life in which she has been investing all along. Her security is based on a secret investment in her appearance and in all that might enhance it. This is the trick that must be kept from being revealed.

This interpretation led the patient to say, with great difficulty because she felt critical of herself for being mean, that the price the analyst had proposed for the session was higher by twenty per cent than she herself charges for an hour of financial consultancy, and that this thought was the first to occur when the analyst mentioned the fee she wanted.

References

Aulagnier, P. (1986). *Un interprèt en quete de signification*. Paris: Éditions Ramsay.

Bion, W. R. (1967). Attacks on linking. In: *Second Thoughts* (pp. 93–109). New York: Jason Aronson.

Bion, W. R. (1992). *Cogitations*. London: Karnac.

Britton, R. (1998). *Belief and Psychic Reality. Belief and Imagination*. London: Routledge.

Da Rocha Barros, E. (1997). O pictograma afetivo. Unpublished manuscript.

Da Rocha Barros, E. M. (2000). Affect and pictographic image: the constitution of meaning in mental life. *International Journal of Psychoanalysis, 81*: 1087–1099.

Dodds, E. R. (1965). *Les Grecs et l'irrationnel*. Paris: Flamarion [*The Greeks and the Irrational*. Berkeley, Los Angeles and Oxford: University of California Press, 1962].

Fédida, P. (1996). *O Sítio do Estrangeiro*. São Paulo: Ed. Escuta.

Ferro, A. (1995). *A Técnica na Psicanálise Infantil*. Rio de Janeiro: Imago.

Ferro, A. (1999). *The Bi-Personal Field: Experiences in Child Analysis*. Routledge: London and New York.

Klein, M. (1975). *Love, Guilt and Reparation: And Other Works 1921-1945*. London: The Hogarth Press and the Institute of Psychoanalysis.

Mancia, M. (1989). *El sueño como religión de la mente*. Madrid: Tecnipublicaciones.

Melsohn, I. (1989). Sentido, significação, sonho. *Revista Brasileira de Psicanálise, 23*(3): 55–70.

Meltzer, D. (1984). *Dream-Life: A Re-examination of the Psychoanalytic Theory and Technique*. Oxford: Clunie Press.

Meyer, L. (2014). Nono fórum teórico clínico: sonhos. (Trabalho apresentado na SBPSP em 13/03/2014-Ainda não publicado).

O'Shaughnessy, E. (2011). Relating to the superego. In: C. Mawson (Ed.), *Bion Today* (pp. 173–187). London: Routledge.

Palombo, S. (1978). The adaptative function of dreams. *Psychoanalysis and Contemporary Thought, 1*: 443–476.

Resnik, S. (1984). *El teatro del sueño*. Madrid: Tecnipublicaciones.

Siqueira, M. (1991). Resenha do Livro *Dream Life* by D. Meltzer,) in *Revista Brasileira de Psicanálise, 25*: 766–767 [Review of the book *Dream Life* by D. Meltzer, in *Brazilian Journal of Psychoanalysis, 25*: 766–767].

Stolorow, R. D., & Atwood, G. E. (1993). Psychoanalytic phenomenology of the dream. In: S. Flanders (Ed.), *The Dream Discourse Today*. London: Routledge.

Stokes, A. (1972). *The Image in Form: Selected Writings of Adrian Stokes*, R. Wollheim (Ed.). London: Penguin.

CHAPTER SIX

Attacks on linking in parents of young disturbed children

Christine Anzieu-Premmereur

The work of Bion has enabled analysts to understand the significance of the impact of emotional factors on the process of developing a capacity for thoughts, in early development as in the analytic setting.

Early in life, this function is provided by the mother's capacity for reverie, when she is available to receive the infant's primitive feelings. For Bion, the mother experiences these feelings mostly as the fear of the baby's dying; it is her ability to regain a balanced state of mind that will enable the transformation of the baby's chaotic emotions into organized ones, which can then be named and thought. A mother who is insufficiently open to the baby's communication, or overwhelmed by it, will not be able to tolerate this process. She will create defences against the flow of emotions that will interfere with the dyadic interaction as a primary impairment that could be a source of pathological communication between parent and child. The disorganisation experienced by some fragile mothers post-partum after a difficult conception, pregnancy, or birth, and the vulnerability of some infants, can sometimes fill the emotional encounter between mother and newborn with turbulence.

Both parents could regress to their own narcissistic and oedipal issues when they become parents, or when they are faced with an inconsolable baby, or an infant who does not satisfy their ideal. When the child shows signs of disorder, the wounded parent develops primitive defences.

Paranoid attitudes and transferential attacks from parents are part of the work of the child analyst. The parents' vulnerability to their child's unconscious processes, and their sensitivity towards the child analyst's intervention, can make the interaction between parents and therapist very difficult at times. Some parents who are dealing with perinatal issues might develop a psychotic transference with pathological splitting, confusional states, and a primitive superego that leads to a negative transference, where the analyst is experienced as an omnipotent, sadistic figure who is judgemental and critical. Violent reproaches and actions can make the analyst feel helpless, angry, and crushed by accusation, experiencing in his turn in the countertransference the pain and the narcissistic injury that some parents project into him.

Bion emphasised the destructiveness directed against the relatedness to the object: this aggression is not only intrapsychic, but also interpersonal, as we observe in psychotic reactions to the birth of a child, when the projections into the baby are pathological and highly aggressive. Bion's concept of the death instinct is the fear of dying: that is, the infant's agony which the mother receives, feels, contains, and transforms into messages so that a translation into meaning takes place. The requirement to bear and absorb this experience of fear of dying puts some parents at risk of disorganisation. The parental imagination plays an essential role in this theory. Psychotic projections from parents interfere with the child's capacity for symbolisation. The parent, being "the thinker who thinks the thoughts", as Grotstein wrote in 1981, "the dreamer who dreams the dream", is a receptive mind that can associate familiarity with the unfamiliar experience. The "digestive alchemy of transformation" is an unconscious creative process of imagination, not an intellectual capacity. The capacity for thinking is there at its source.

Some parents have negative reactions to the child's reality, and will eventually project into the child analyst their despair and narcissistic conflicts. I have observed, in parents presenting themselves as well regulated, loving, and caring adults, moments of psychotic reactions that I thought were associated with the child's disturbance and aggravated by it: dissociation and states of emptiness, with destructive impulses, states of chaos, panic and splitting, acting out, and lack of memory of those reactions. All those difficult events were attacks on the child's ability for bonding or to be attached to the object, on the analyst's capacity for thinking, and on the setting of the therapy.

As we know from Bion, attacks are reactions to a countertransference that prevented the analyst from being receptive to the projections, insensitive to the emotions in the relationship. If the parents have experienced the child analyst as having an intellectual curiosity towards them that is not based on emotional exchange, an "arrogant" attitude, they develop a mostly non-verbal communication that will induce in the analyst an emotional experience similar to theirs.

Parents often feel that they are being hurt by consulting for symptoms in their child; some experience this as being "cheated" and have hostile reactions. Persecutory feelings, envy, and hatred are projected in the consulting room. The analyst might feel that she is under attack and be willing to interpret this, when it is a part object relationship that is at the core of this paranoid phase. Bion reminded us that the splitting of the guilt made the patient unable to think. Projective identification is at work, and the analyst is being used to receive and experience "the feelings of resentment at the deprivation" due to the analyst's refusal to accept parts of their personality (Bion, 1967, p. 96).

Helplessness in parents dealing with an inconsolable baby, an autistic toddler, or a fragile child with developmental delay, puts some of them in the position of a child waiting for containment. The narcissistic injury in presenting to the analyst a child who can no longer be an ideal part of themselves made them frightened of him because of their violent projective identification.

This impasse is complicated by the fact that the paradoxical communication that is often part of the verbal exchange with the analyst is also present towards the child.

The mother will say that she cannot stand her child any more and cannot understand him, while the child will react with intense emotional discharge. The analyst who witnesses the parent's failure will be accused of insensitivity. Bion wrote,

> My deduction was that in order to understand what the child wanted the mother should have treated the infant's cry as more than a

demand for her presence. From the infant's point of view she should have taken into her, and thus experienced, the fear that the child was dying. It was that fear that the child could not contain. An understanding mother is able to experience the feeling of dread, that this baby was striving to deal with by projective identification and yet retain a balanced outlook. Bion, 1967, p. 95)

The tendency to excessive projective identification is reinforced when the mother is unable to contain the projections. Another consequence is the failure to introject, which Bion pointed out as the cause of early development of the superego in the form of a severe, destructive superego. Fuelled by envy and greed, this harsh superego develops when the infant is unable to get satisfaction from, and to satisfy, the object. Bion develops this important idea that the failure to introject projective identification "makes the external object appear intrinsically hostile to curiosity" (1967, p. 98).

The internal object is felt to be opposed to links and communication, and to be mostly destructive of links. The links are more attached to functions than to an object, and this makes the consequence of the attack very severe: there is a serious risk of arrested development when lack of curiosity interferes with cognitive and emotional development. The absence of the capacity to think is understood as the consequence of a catastrophic experience in which the feelings that the child wished to deposit into the mother were ejected. Therefore, every good, understanding object must be destroyed. Since the disaster was not experienced as a state, but as a dynamic process, there is a continuous process of projecting the fantasy of coupling parents "engaged in a creative act . . . at sharing an enviable emotional experience" (1967, p. 92).

Creativity is transformed into hostile destruction. This is what Bion observes in the difficult analysis with patients presenting psychotic personalities. Child analysts and those working with parents and babies in the same room made the same observations.

Attacks on linking might occur in new mothers suffering from a psychotic reaction to the birth of their child, in parents presenting a psychotic part of their personality that is actualised in the transference, and in the negative transference in narcissistic, vulnerable parents who are unable to face their child's troubles.

This shows how analytic understanding of maternal unconscious function and babies' primitive anxieties, defences, and need for containment allow the analyst to use interpretations and interventions that help the baby to decrease the tension and gain libidinal pleasure.

An inconsolable baby refusing the breast

This is an example of direct intervention with a baby after a therapeutic alliance has been made with the mother and the father. The analyst works to activate parts of the infant's inner world that had been excluded from containment, so that the emotional disturbance can be worked through in the mother–infant relationship.

Tina is only a few weeks old. She was born after insemination with the father's sperm and egg from a donor. The mother felt weird during the pregnancy and cried for help after the much-wanted baby was born, because she felt unable to connect to Tina. The newborn was already an active baby looking for contact, avid for eye-to-eye interaction with the father and the analyst, but avoiding the mother's look. The mother's ambivalence towards a child that reminded her of the narcissistic wound of her infertility had brought the dyad to an impasse. At first, Tina was able to take the breast while avoiding the mother's eyes. But, three weeks later, she stopped actively sucking the nipple while crying and screaming. The mother felt depressed and desperate about feeding her daughter. After twenty-four hours of huge anxiety and refusal to open her mouth for either breast or bottle, Tina was able to drink the mother's milk from a bottle when in the father's arms. She became an inconsolable baby, screaming for hours.

While I talked to the mother about her anguish at not being able to love the child and be loved by her, we associated this with her rage towards her husband, who could legitimately claim to be the parent of the baby while she felt she was not; I talked about the egg donor as a rival and she immediately associated with her anger towards her own mother, who claims that Tina always smiled at her.

She thought she had been a difficult baby herself and had made her own mother suffer a lot, and she was afraid of having, in her turn, an infant who would "abuse" her, to whom she submitted passively. She was obsessed with persecutory ideas about the baby's needs. Her husband was unable to help her, since he disconnected from her in "blank moments" when she was panicking.

Baby Tina is on the couch, looking intensely towards the mother, and turning her head when she meets the mother's eyes. I ask about the events of the day she had stopped sucking the breast, and her mother bursts into tears while remembering that was the day her own parents came to visit the family, and she felt enraged. She feels so guilty, and envious of the father's capacity to feed the baby.

Tina is agitated and looks for some containment, I tell her that mummy is sad and angry, and that made her frightened. Since the mother agrees with me and has said she was ashamed of those weird feelings, I ask her to take Tina to console her and not to be afraid of her baby, who needs to love her but was afraid of her face and her emotions felt through the skin contact. The mother is very interested, and, after long minutes of intense screaming, Tina calms down in her mother's arms.

The mother described her feelings of exclusion and loss, after the loss of her illusion that she could be seen by her husband as a good mother. She was very anxious about giving birth to a baby that she felt as being different, since she would always see the signs of the other woman, the egg donor, who was a stranger; she had her first association during a session with her fear of losing her mother when she was five and her sister was born. The baby would be at risk of evoking the loss of her mother and the loss of a mirroring function. So, when Tina avoided her eyes, she thought this proved her inability to attract the attention of others.

She was also afraid that her ties with her husband had weakened dangerously. The role distribution between the parents was very rigid and the father tended to adopt the role of an ideal parent who was controlling the dyad. The mother had developed a masochistic attitude to parenting, submissively and dutifully acting like a perfect mother, but without pleasure. She saw her husband as the ideal parent and the infant as a rival to be removed. The couple was at risk of severe conflict in dealing with a reciprocal projective identification system of parental objects that were disappointing, frustrating, persecuting, and functioning in superego mode at a time when she experienced the baby as demanding a strongly idealised parental role.

Many sessions were marked by the same painful development, while I suffered the experience of the baby's distress and the mother's anxiety about being able to feel good at calming Tina. Each time, I was able to catch the baby's eyes and to talk directly to her, while explaining to her and her mother that they both experienced the same fear. One day, the mother came with the wish to resume breastfeeding her daughter, since she had regained some trust in her maternal capacity. Tina is screaming, but she looks to her mother with quick glances while crying. The mother cries also, and tries to give her nipple to the baby, who abruptly turns her head away. There is violence in that scene that suggests to me a conflict in the baby between the drives' urges to be fed, the fear of engaging with the depressed mother, and the impulse to destroy the breast. I remember Winnicott's decision (Winnicott & Hügel, 1967) to put his hand between a four-month-old baby's mouth and the breast, but I am not secure enough to act. I interpret directly to the baby the repressed hate for the mother, and we see the infant's affect storms.

I ask the mother to touch Tina's head in a gentle way and to talk to her. The touching immediately calms the baby who looks at me and then slowly turns her head towards the mother. The mother then becomes active: smiling at Tina for the first time, she says with a firm voice, "It's time to drink, Tina, I am here for you." She decides to put the nipple into the baby's mouth herself while looking at me with a smile, and the baby begins to suck, quite slowly, until the moment when she regains her avidity and her pleasure at being fed.

I quote Winnicott:

> The self essentially recognizes itself in the eyes and facial expression of the mother and in the mirror, which can come to represent the mother's face. Eventually the self arrives at a significant relationship between the child and the sum of the identification, after enough incorporation and introjection of mental representations, become organized in the shape of an internal psychic living reality. . . . It is the self and the life of the self that alone makes sense of action or of living . . . and of the capacity to identify with mature love objects without loss of individual identity. (1971, p. 48)

For Winnicott, the trauma is represented by the need to react instead of being. The extreme sense of insecurity, the loss of continuity of the self, the threat of annihilation, could lead to the first ego organisation if repeatedly the experience is that of recovery, but if the mother fails to adapt to the infant's needs, there will be annihilation of the infant's sense of self, the risk of acute confusion, or agony of disintegration.

The immense fragility of the early development stresses the essential role of mutuality of the relationship, the experience of being held, handled, seen and met in a creative gesture. Intimacy can be destroyed by overwhelming emotions.

As Bion emphasised, such a disturbance in the relationship to the mother causes an early development of the superego. The baby's refusal of the breast, even when very hungry, has been interpreted by Winnicott as precocious superego activity (1967).

Libidinisation of the body is essential to protect the very young baby against the consequences of traumatic experiences that lead to anxiety, accumulation of aggression, rage, and attacks associated with self-destructiveness. The physical interpenetration of nipple and mouth together with the emotional interpenetration mediated by the eyes can lead to harmonious embodiment of the self. But some babies experience states of catastrophic unintegration, which have not been healed by the mother's reverie. The countertransference during the screaming sessions was an experience of repetition of the pathological scenario when two fragile people cannot reach each other, fail to stay unified, and lose their sense of self in a massive experience of disorganisation full of persecution and anguish.

The early development of the superego is also a consequence of the mother's inability to receive and transform the anxiety and the destructiveness that the child is experiencing and needs to discharge. The consequence is the development of a persecutory object that exercises the function of a destructive superego, and the inability to face the depressive position, as shown by Bion:

> The link between infant and breast depends upon projective identification and a capacity to introject projective identifications. Failure to introject makes the external object appear intrinsically hostile to curiosity and to the method, namely projective identification, by which the infant seeks to satisfy it. Should the breast be felt as fundamentally understanding, it has been transformed by the infant's envy and hate into an object whose devouring greed has as its aim the introjection of the infant's projective identifications in order to destroy them. This can show in the patient's belief that the analyst strives, by understanding the patient, to drive him insane. The result is an object which, when installed in the patient, exercises the function of a severe and ego-destructive superego. (1967, p. 98)

The psychoanalyst works with babies and their parents in direct intervention with the infant, using interpretation that is based on the understanding of the child's early ego function and specific defences, and on the effects of the infant's emotions on the mother, the "wild things", and "anxiety that can rise as shared wildness provides evidence of potential destructiveness" (Raphael-Leff, 2005, p. 291).

Paranoid reactions in the parents of three-year-old Ella

Ella is a tiny, three-year-old girl who is unable to comply with the school's daily routine. She defies all the rules and lies on the floor obsessively joining two toys, mostly animals, together with string. If she cannot have string or rope, she could scream for hours. She is the first child of a young couple; the father is a very active, proud man with narcissistic reactions, on the edge of persecutory reactions. The mother is a soft, shy woman, easily confused and lost in time and space, who had experienced being disorganised, and, I thought, sometimes dissociated, in the post partum period, when she could scream at her crying infant. She began to do better as soon as she returned to work. Both parents say they strongly believe in therapy, with idealisation and a lack of thinking. After many consultations and parent–child sessions, I started psychoanalysis with Ella. She entered treatment with great interest; I soon became her "very best friend" and she reported that she had been "dead" sometimes when she was a baby.

As we explore abandonment fears, rage, and guilt while playing together at attaching animals with string, Ella begins to develop better language skills, and a new curiosity about the external world. Some days, she can be frozen in a state of withdrawal and depression, sucking her thumb and lying on the couch, avoiding contact. I finally realise that those moments happen on specific days, when the baby-sitter is not available and the mother brings her to the session.

The game of splitting bad and good animals develops; those who are mean have to stay in a specific closed area. Finally, after months of treatment, she introduces human characters into the play. Binding together mother and daughter takes hours, and a father figure stays around.

When I started to feel some relief at the thought that Ella's development was getting back on track and became more creative with imaginary scenarios of oedipal figures, she started to miss sessions. The mother became confused about the schedule; she forgot to come or to tell the baby-sitter, or she sent Ella at the wrong time. When Ella appeared many times in the waiting room on days or hours when she was not supposed to come, I felt confused, sad, angry, and helpless, facing the disappointed child who had lost the secure setting of the sessions and her confidence in me. During the missed sessions, when I was waiting and calling the mother in vain, my countertransference was of aggressive reactions and impotence. When Ella came at the wrong time and looked at me in despair, I felt helpless with chaotic depressive emotions and guilt. It took me minutes to reorganise myself and find words to re-establish contact with Ella and to find a solution when I could.

The frame had been attacked; Ella had been late fourteen times in three months, missing ten sessions and coming six times at the wrong time. Both parents denied the missed sessions and any wrongdoing. Interpreting the mother's ambivalence and rivalry with me was received with a smiling denial. She finally came with the father, very late, to the session that I have been requesting for many weeks, saying that her mind had been "elsewhere" and that she was disconnected from reality. She was surprised that I was annoyed by the changes in the sessions' schedule. The father accused me of being inflexible, very strict and judgemental. I had billed for the missed sessions, but he denied that these sessions had been missed and claimed that they had not been due to come. He was in a rage and violently accused me of abusing patients in front of others in the waiting room, which embarrassed and silenced me.

It had never occurred to the mother that her confusion could have consequences for her daughter. I told her about my waiting for her and her phone call, and she was able to agree with my idea that she was experiencing my needing her, with the association that she had the wish that I would ask her to continue the relationship. This was the first session with an associative process, when she remembered her screaming at her own mother when she was a child but was not heard by her and felt unloved and unimportant to both her parents. I tried to show her that Ella's screaming when she was a toddler asking her to stay was a repetition of the same scene. She was sad when she told me that she knew she could not stand her daughter's neediness and wanted to flee from her. A new therapeutic alliance was being established; Ella returned for regular sessions.

The father then asked for consultation, complaining about my abusive behaviour and inadequate judgement, since I was supposed to have said to his wife that parents were responsible for the child's issues. After idealising me as "the best therapist in the city", who would transform wife and daughter into successful people he could be proud of, I deeply disappointed him and even attacked him. Arrogance was followed by misery, and contemplating a feeling of guilt made him very aggressive. Ella was like a narcissistic part of himself and a source of his pride. But he received a letter from the school with details about Ella's symptoms that made him furious, and he thought I had damaged his daughter. The persecutory feelings that filled the room were about bad women, a neglecting mother figure, weak child, and a mix of castrated female and bad maternal figures. He had experienced fear of Ella's death, perhaps for the first time, when the school reported about a drawing of a rotten flower by Ella, which she said was "in order to learn more about death". I told him how anxious he and his wife were about Ella's sadness. After some turmoil, I was able to give the mother a referral to start therapy.

But the paradoxical communication with the father lasted a while, since he denied the missed sessions and did not want to pay for them. He said the child had attended all the sessions in question and at the same time denied that he had to pay for them. Whatever I said was proof of my abusing the family, my greed and selfishness. He already had given me the payment and wanted me to reimburse him.

I felt miserable, with a strong resentment, and ashamed to have shown my inability to manage the situation well and my psychoanalytic inability to understand and to protect Ella. I had the wish that they would not come back and would find another analyst instead. My sense of guilt was intense. I thought that this form of paradoxical communication must be part of the family dynamics and needed to be explored. I remembered the French analyst, Racamier (1973, p. 663), who said "logical paradoxes are forms of the death instinct". The negative narcissism and the paranoid anxiety were part of Ella's upbringing. Denial and destruction of the libidinal bond that underlies the therapeutic alliance with the child were part of the negative transference and the guilt projected into me. I understood the massive repression of aggressive impulse towards the object, in both the mother and the father, the idealisation and superego figures that had taken the central role in the parent–child relationship, and the need to deny any depressed feelings. I thought they all needed an object of containment, and decided to tell them that I wanted to continue to see Ella and to see them on a regular basis to give them an opportunity to express their concerns. I also said that the way they talked to me, the mother with a cold detachment and the father with violent anger, was a sign of their suffering, and also, perhaps, their reactions in the past in front of their own parents. Memories and fantasies about neglect, abandonment, and rejection from parental figures followed my suggestion. I strongly opposed their judgement that I was only interested in money and my (narcissistic) assurance calmed the father down for a while.

The capacity for "linking" was restored momentarily, and we set up appointments for sessions as a "thinking team" for Ella. She immediately benefited from this change and her behaviour at school improved a lot. The string obsession diminished and finally disappeared to make room for an appetite to learn, since she developed quite a precocious interest in reading and writing; she was almost five. In sessions, she started to bring scenarios and some libidinal pleasure.

However, each holiday break caused a regression, the mother disorganising the frame, the father having bouts of violence, and the child starting compulsive masturbation. Absence made them desperate, with the parents attacking the analysis and Ella destroying her work at school. Experiencing their vacation as my absence, and the loss of an idealised support, they could not face any depressive feelings, and attacked the analytic work as a source of envy, a symbolic equivalent of the breast as the establishment of linkage. Maintaining the frame, the continuity of the treatment, the child's transference, the value of symbols and language was hard work. The mother denied that her daughter was able to read, and we had another difficult time when she decided to switch the therapy to meet with a behavioural specialist who would operate on her daughter like a mechanic on her brain. Nevertheless, I was able maintain the analysis for the next two years, until the parents decided to terminate, at a point when Ella was autonomous enough to show her anger towards them.

Anzieu (1986) described the paradoxical communication as a negative illusion. He gave an example very close to what I observed in Ella's family, of parents denying what a child actually felt:

> "Your sensation of the bath being too hot is a false one; that is what you say, but it is not true that you feel it; parents know better than children what the children feel, and neither your body nor your truth belong to you", the parents were no longer on moral grounds of good and bad. They were on the logical grounds of the confusion between true and false and their paradox was to oblige the child to invent or exchange true and false. From this stem the consecutive difficulties in the constitution of ego boundaries and of reality, and in the communication to others of one's point of view. Good and bad are contradictory notions and the corresponding logic applies essentially to wishes, desires. The confusion between true and false produces another logic which goes beyond desire influencing sensation, perception, memory, judgment, and, more generally thought . . . The paradoxical relation between mother (or father) and child is symmetrically reversed as in the state described by Winnicott (1951) as that of transitional phenomena and of illusion, in which is established a link of trust between mother, ego, and the world, and the possibility to establish, through thinking, correspondences between external reality and internal reality. Paradox, on the contrary, favors defiance and splitting. This kind of relating subverts the sense of truth and of the subject's very being. I propose to define this paradoxical relation as the negative illusion. She was then no longer sure of her own sensations, ideas and desires. The limits of her ego became blunted. (Anzieu, 1986, p. 525).

The destructiveness of a paradox in the communication between parents and child was recognised in Fairbairn's (1952) description of the core of the schizoid position. The child "feels that the reason for her (the mother) apparent refusal to accept his love is that his own love is destructive and bad" (p. 25).

In the paradoxical situation, the superego remains confused with the ego-ideal and the drive investment it receives comes from the death instinct. The insufficient autonomy of the ego and the omnipotence of the superego prevent the establishment of the pleasure–unpleasure and the reality principles.

> The psychic apparatus falls prey to a third principle, the reduction of tensions to their lowest level. This means that in lieu of developing an

> élan for living with its moments of fullness, joy, creation, there develops a substitute for a sort of dismal and relatively impersonal subexistence. With these patients, the liberal analytic situation instead of fostering the liberation of repressed and inhibited aggression, as it classically does with neurotics, exacerbates their self-destructiveness. (Anzieu, 1986, p. 526)

Classical psychoanalytic understanding will always fail in these conflicts. Only the countertransference of bitterness and the feeling of failure can alert the analyst to the quality of the transference, and provide information about the parents' feelings and projections.

This is also the view of Green on the radical destructiveness of negative narcissism, when it leads to decathexis, a general disobjectalising function.

Absence was the starting point whenever there was a crisis with the parents, while for Ella that absence felt like death. Absence is an intermediate situation between presence—with the risk of intrusive presence—and total loss that can imply destruction. The intensity of the parents' reaction to any interruption in sessions which occurred due to their absence but was experienced as their being deprived showed me the "work of the negative". Instead of symbolic displacement of an object felt as present, they had developed a world with no meaning with the urge to destroy any process that would provide meaning and link to the absent object. I observed in the mother, and the father described, what Green described as "catastrophic or unthinkable anxieties, fears of annihilation or breakdown, feelings of futility, of devitalization, or of psychic death, sensations of a gap, of bottomless holes, of an abyss" (Green, 1999, p. 84), such as is manifested in acute forms of depression or ego disintegration.

The consequences for the young child's psyche are crucial. When objectalisation's integrative function is opposed, investment in objects, facilitating relations between subject and object and binding are weakened. Green insisted,

> It is not only the object which is cathected, but the activity of investment itself. It is the investment of investment that creates greater and greater areas of integration and linking. Disobjectalization, on the contrary, leads to psychic discontinuity, to splitting, fragmentation and disorganization. Not only the object relation but whatever substitutes for it, including the investment itself, finds itself under attack by the unbinding of this function. (Reed & Baudry, 2005, p. 124)

Early depression in babies, seen in apathy, relational detachment, sometimes in avoidance or psychosomatic disorganisation, is associated with problematic narcissistic parenting. The lack of bonding between infant and parents becomes hyper attachment in compensation. Mood disorders follow and, during his second year, the child can develop forms of autism and/or delay in the development of communication and symbolic activities.

Autistic defences in a four-year-old boy facing parental narcissistic issues and projections

Bob is almost four and had been expelled from school after two weeks, since he was running non-stop in the classroom and licking the teacher's shoes during reading time. His parents were shocked, denying any wrongdoing in their first child, though he had been diagnosed already with a developmental disorder a year before, with autistic signs. They reported a history of perfect benign development, but the mother had been very distressed by anxiety and had had difficulties with touching the newborn or holding him; she had the fear that he would die, and at the same time she was struggling to face the separation from her own mother, who was moving to another city. On two occasions, Bob presented loss of consciousness that the mother interpreted as sudden infant death syndrome, giving reality to her fear, but those crises were actually diagnosed as sobbing spasms, or breath-holding spells, which have a more psychosomatic origin and are associated with the mother's anxiety: they are paroxysms in which the baby's vigorous crying is followed by a brief period of apnoea, pallor, and loss of consciousness for a few seconds. The mother was unable to separate from the baby after these crises, which occurred around the time when her own mother had moved out of the city.

Since mother and baby were very close, "almost symbiotic" said the father, he decided to impose a very strict separation by giving twelve-month-old Bob to his own mother in a faraway village, unknown to the toddler, for two weeks, so that the mother could resume working and, at the same time, the child would be weaned from the breast and able to sleep independently. Bob cried and screamed non-stop for many days, and finally took a bottle and slept by himself. When the parents returned to pick him up, he avoided them and had maintained a total detachment from them ever since. The boy's withdrawal was interpreted by the father as a success, but Bob had completely stopped playing and was not developing any auto-erotic or transitional function.

After some sessions with mother and child, I assessed Bob as a child with a developmental delay and a few autistic defences, and I decided to start therapy. The first session, when he had to leave his mother in the waiting room, he looked at me intensely for the first time, put his fingers in his mouth and held his breath. I was very impressed by his compulsion to use his body to inflict pain on it and to threaten me with death anxiety. I told him I did not want him to do that any more, that I understood his fear at losing his mummy, but that he was all right and could not harm himself. After a long, silent break, he said, "Mummy is sad." We started talking about his parents' feelings, drawing their faces when sad or angry, and playing, to the extent that he was able to focus his attention.

Several authors have emphasised the importance of combining touch and sight with infants. Anzieu, in *The Skin Ego* (1989), showed how gazing associated with skin contact puts the mother in contact with her psychic reality while longing for mutual incorporation with her baby. The narcissistic "seduction" based on sensory experience, united in the body ego, depends upon maternal reverie's capacity for receiving the primitive emotional states projected by the baby.

Grotstein's work on the background object of primary identification concerned experiences of depersonalisation connected with the background support:

> The background object of primary identification is the guardian of inchoate constancy from the very beginning of life until representation of objects can replace the presentation of object (self object, internal object), allowing for transformation of the background object into a deity-like concept associated with a super ego and ego ideal. (Grotstein, 1981, p. 80)

The pathological decathexis of the object that Green described in his 1993 paper, The dead mother", is observed in avoidant babies who eventually develop into toddlers with autistic defences, for whom a sudden noise is terrifying, as if it signalled the brutal appearance of the absent and denied object.

Bob's critical reaction to noise was regulated when he was able to make eye contact with me and I was joking about bad witches invading the room, and associating the fear with the absence of the mother. Genevieve Haag quote Frances Tustin:

> The brutality with which an object that has left the background suddenly reappears, when a psychic trauma is due to premature awareness of bodily separation, yielding a sense of skin torn off and prompting a ceaseless search for a single skin for two people. (Dubinsky et al., 1997, p. 206)

Establishing a sense of body boundaries and internal connectedness will lay the foundation for a secure sense of self. The child was constantly searching for fusion, through adhesive identification or massive destructive projective identification. The analyst's role is to endure the violence and despair of the young patient. In spite of trauma and pathological interactions that disrupt the therapy, most of them have kept a life-seeking strength that helps to maintain an established sense of self, and a transference ambivalent enough to maintain the contact with the analyst. Bob must have experienced states of catastrophic unintegration, which were not healed by the mother's reverie. The countertransference with him was sometimes very painful.

The maternal function was impaired by the mother's own separation issues and huge anxiety, so they did not present a picture of a solid, perfect, dyadic union, but the paternal function, as an introduction to a symbolic order, did not provide Bob with a solid support.

The father, with his own serious issues and narcissistic negative projections into his son, wanted to perform a paternal function and thought it was important to work on separation, but his own unconscious hatred towards mother figures made him sever all the links he could detect between Bob and any female presence and he aggressively destroyed all the efforts made to reorganise the disturbed child. The dyadic system with mother and the grandmother was experienced as a couple that was excluding him, the father, and the same applied to the relationship between Bob and his analyst. He made impulsive rage-filled choices whose negative consequences he denied; this was a pattern I had to face during the therapy. Every choice we agreed on during the parents' consultations with me, about school, baby-sitting, education, special help or leisure for his son—after tons of emails from the anxious mother—were negated the next day. For example, after I had worked to secure a place for Bob in a very attentive, well-contained school with few young children in one classroom, speaking Bob's family language, Bob was registered a week later in a school where he could not speak his mother tongue and was unable to understand anything for six months, during which he regressed to more autistic features.

This was a total "confusion of tongues". It took me a while to understand the father's needs and to contain his destructive behaviour that he was unaware of. When I saw his own need to be a child and offered him the opportunity to attend some sessions when he could play with his son, I observed that he took all the toys for himself without paying attention to me and forgetting his son. Bob was a rival into whom he had projected negative representations of a greedy, dangerous, aggressive character that was a source of persecution and needed to be controlled. Intense guilt feelings were associated with these persecutory projections. Through projective identification, I received a distant, rejecting, hostile object. For a long time, the decisions the father made were concerned only to erase the mother's choices or annul the therapy sessions. This was always done by email, never by talking to me. Each time, Bob became more withdrawn and destroyed his drawings or the toys he used to like.

Negative transference associated with destructive behaviour was described by Espasa and colleagues as typical of narcissistic–dissociated parenting conflicts. When the parents make pathological projective identifications on to their infant, they usually use the same pathological defence mechanisms towards the therapist and often establish a "negative pre-transference". The intense persecutory feelings experienced by these parents are mostly denied and are very destructive, both to their interactions with their infant and to their own mental activity.

> The "negative pre-transference" provokes negative countertransference reactions regarding the parents. The therapist frequently identifies himself with the baby and tends to judge the parents negatively. However, the work of the therapist is not only the child and the parental conflict, but the parents' sufferings as well. In order to do this work, it is important to take the complaints of the parents seriously

> and to give them equal priority with the symptomatic manifestations of the baby. It is a long and tortuous process in order to work on their past mourning processes against which the parents defend themselves in a radical and projective manner. (Espasa et al., 1999, p. 473)

The countertransference is an essential tool to allow the analyst to feel the anger and helplessness of parents dealing with narcissistic suffering while facing their child's primitive anxiety or pathological reactions. To return to a capacity of reverie, the analyst resumes the sensation-based, proto-symbolic activity that makes him or her emotionally present as an analyst, aware of the empty space of the negative narcissism that is fuelling paranoid reactions and destructiveness. There is no way to avoid feeling the anguish associated with the attacks on linking. Reacting without arrogance and rejection is a goal. Another goal is the libidinisation of the interactions with children in analysis or dyadic therapy: to stay in conjunction with infantile sexuality, to maintain the conditions for the emergence of creativity, while dealing with aggression in the transference, even with very young children and babies.

There are serious consequences for the child's capacity for thinking when they are faced with parental defence mechanisms against paranoid and depressive feelings. Some mothers are in a state of panic, offering a chaotic holding or regressing into a psychic retreat when the perinatal period is too stressful and new to them. The parasitic action of narcissistic parental projections makes working with young children an important but challenging task, and Bion's understanding of attacks on linking offers a very important orientating perspective to help the analyst to face and try to resolve those impasses. When strict limit setting associated with benevolent neutrality in the analyst's response to the parent's destructive behaviour enables a therapeutic alliance to be maintained, the feeling of helplessness in parents leaves room for a sense of agency to develop and could help the child to regain some libidinal exposure to the relationship with the parents. Spontaneous humour and the resumption of dreaming in depressed and persecuted parents are the best indicators of a new capacity to recognise contradiction, incoherence, ambiguity, and paradox.

References

Anzieu, D. (1986). Paradoxical transference—from paradoxical communication to negative therapeutic reaction. *Contemporary Psychoanalysis, 22*: 520–547.

Anzieu, D. (1989). *The Skin Ego*. New Haven, CT: Yale University Press.

Bion, W. R. (1967). *Second Thoughts: Selected Papers on Psychoanalysis* (pp. 93–110). London: Heinemann.

Dubinsky, A., Dubinsky, H., Rhode, M., & Rustin, M. (1997). *Psychotic States in Children*. London: Karnac.

Espasa, F. P., Manzano, J., & Zilkha, N. (1999). The narcissistic scenarios of parenthood. *International Journal of Psychoanalysis, 80*(3): 465–476.

Fairbairn, W. R. D. (1952). An object-relations theory of personality. In: *Psychoanalytic Studies of the Personality* (pp. 3–28). London: Tavistock Publications Ltd.

Green, A. (1993). The dead mother. *Psyche, 47*(3): 205–240.

Green, A. (1999). *The Work of the Negative*, A. Weller (Trans.). London: Free Association.

Grotstein, J. S. (1981). Primal splitting, the background object of primacy identification and other self-objects. In: *Splitting and Projective Identification* (pp. 77–89). New York: Aronson.

Racamier, P. C. (1973). Entre humour et folie. *Revue Français de Psychanalyse, 37*: 655–668.

Raphael-Leff, J. (2005). Parent–infant psychodynamics: wild things, mirrors and ghosts. *Infant Observation, 8*(3): 291–292.

Reed, G. S., & Baudry, F. D. (2005). Conflict, structure, and absence: André Green on borderline and narcissistic pathology. *Psychoanalytic Quarterly, 74*: 121–155.

Winnicott, D. W. (1971). Lettre adressée à la *Revue Française de Psychanalyse* (Letter to the *Revue Française*). Personal translation, 3, p. 48.

Winnicott, D. W., & Hügel, K. (1967). Eine Kinderbeobachtung. *Psyche, 21*(10–11): 848–852.

CHAPTER SEVEN

An interrupted treatment[1]

Monica Horovitz

> "My violent inclination seduced me . . . and I felt that you were less dear to me than my passion"
>
> (De La Vergne, *Letters of the Portuguèse Nun*, 1669)

A treatment that is suddenly interrupted is a shared traumatic experience, even if it is not immediately recognised or perceived as such. New light is shed retrospectively on the patient and his or her analytic trajectory, revealing resistances or weaknesses that were hitherto unsuspected. Any analyst who has experienced such an impact will be sensitive to the clinical and theoretical interest of an investigation and reflection focused on these stumbling blocks, which, after all, arise quite frequently.

Prelude

In his famous essay of 1959, "Attacks on linking", Bion suggests that, for patients, the analytic relationship is creative, and the unconscious equivalent of the procreative relationship of the parents. As such, it becomes an object of intense envy, jealousy, and aggressiveness concerning "all links whatsoever from the most primitive . . . to the most sophisticated forms of verbal communication and the arts" (1967, p. 108). He adds, "The patient's disposition to attack the link between two objects is simplified because the analyst has to establish a link with the patient and does this by verbal communication and his equipment of psycho-analytical experience" (p. 94).

Owing to the stimulus to think which the analytic situation provides and to the normal degree of projective identification that the transference involves, the patient establishes a relationship, consciously and unconsciously, with the analyst. This is how the analytic couple is formed.

Now some patients react to this formation by splitting: while one part of them seems to be fully engaged in the analytic process (though the narcissistic component of the transference is often predominant), another part seems almost to withdraw from the relationship. This part actively hates the relationship thus formed and contests the transference by denying projections and by refusing any emotional involvement; above all, it directs its attacks against verbal thought, that of associations and interpretations, because its function is to link them together.

The patient attacks his or her own capacity for understanding, the faculty for linking that he or she perceives in the analyst, and also his or her own feelings which are projected on to the analyst with a degree of violence that makes them intolerable for the latter. Bion emphasises that it is not only thinking—in the ordinary sense of the term—that has a linking function in the analytic relationship, but also affect. In the state of splitting I am referring to, emotion becomes an object of hatred to the point that the attacks on its function of linking lead to an excess of fictional links and rationalisations. The remaining links thus seem sterile, while defiance and hatred towards all emotion lead to a hatred for life itself which can even result in a matricide, as outlined further on.

The fundamental tendency towards conflict, antagonism between the drives in favour of the death drive, and also intra-libidinal antagonism—the existence of which Freud (1912d, p. 188) suspected when he suggested that something inherent to the libido might not be favourable to the realisation of complete satisfaction of the sexual drive—are, thus, exalted: the game becomes too unequal and the oscillation between binding and unbinding tips in favour of the latter to the detriment of the former.

This is what Bion expresses in metaphorical terms: hatred reinforces the murderous attacks on what links the analytic pair, on the pair itself, and on the object engendered by the pair. In fact, a sudden and definite rupture often gives the analyst, who is reduced to impotence, the feeling that a murder has taken place, not only of himself and what he represents, but of the analysis itself. The patient has "archaic" reactions to the primal scene and deadly reactions of primary unbinding to the analysis because the analytic pair is experienced as the reincarnation of the parental pair and because the patient feels identified with a spectator baby.

The third party, which is always present in the analytic situation, is not just the parent of the other sex; it is also the analysand/child who is a witness of the scene.

In this situation, then, the patient experiences "a hatred of patent emotion and therefore of life itself. This hatred contributes to the murderous attack on that which links the pair, on the pair itself and on the object generated by the pair" (Bion, 1967, pp. 100–101).

This point of view, which is closer to the experience of an interrupted treatment that I have had and reflected on, is more convincing. Furthermore, this approach, which is in line with the intuitions of Melanie Klein, seems to me to correspond to Freud's last suggestions concerning the splitting of the ego, unlocatable resistances, and the repudiation of femininity in both sexes. Evidence of this may be found in Chapter Eight of *An Outline of Psychoanalysis* (Freud, 1940a) entitled "The psychical apparatus and the external world", where he distinguishes inter- and intrasystemic conflicts. Just as we can observe psychic organisations in which "two attitudes persist side by side throughout their lives without influencing each other" (p. 203), when they are analysed we can see that "the disavowal is always supplemented by an acknowledgement" (p. 204). There would, no doubt, be justification for inverting the formulation and saying that the acknowledgement is always accompanied by a rejection. The transference is, thus, split, torn by contrary psychic attitudes: "The issue depends on which of the two can seize hold of the greater intensity" (p. 204). This takes us back to the economic factor where the prevalence of unbinding implies a disarticulation of the agencies and psychic organisations, and even a partial disintegration within each of them.

At this juncture, I am thinking of the fragmentary but very dense and instructive observation presented by Klein in 1946 to illustrate the connection, rarely noticed, between depressive and schizoid phenomena. It naturally has its place here, since it is centred on the acting out of an interruption. It is worth noting in passing that this acting out occurred at a point "in the course of her analysis [when] a stage was reached in which a real and great improvement was achieved" (1986[1946], p. 16), for this remark coincides with numerous convergent accounts.

The powerful and new resistance shown at this stage seemed to come from only one part of her patient's personality, while at the same time another part continued to respond to the analytic work. Klein writes,

> It was not only that parts of her personality did not co-operate with me; they did not seem to co-operate with each other, and at the time the analysis was unable to help the patient to achieve the synthesis. During this stage she decided to bring the analysis to an end. (1986[1946], p. 17)

This passage circumscribes a disorganising mutation of the psyche, the trying experience of which we have all had. It shows how the primary masochism of certain patients is sometimes reactivated unexpectedly by the links established and the integrations achieved by both the reconstructive and constructive, synthetic and creative, effect of analysis.

While a disarticulation was taking place between the agencies and within the ego itself, the transference relationship became looser and the moment of rupture was approaching quietly. At the end of her analysis, Klein's patient

> came regularly to the analytic sessions, associated fairly freely, reported dreams and provided material for the analysis. There was very seldom any conscious confirmation of what I suggested. Yet the material by which she responded to the interpretations reflected their unconscious effect. (1986[1946], p. 17)

This divorce between conscious and unconscious, this split within the ego between representation and affect, were premonitory signs of a risk of rupture, particularly as this patient had recently been complaining about feelings of inner emptiness, while her therapist observed that her thoughts were losing their coherence, even latent, and that their expression was becoming increasingly disjointed.

These references to Freud, Klein, and Bion elucidate and contribute to structuring the clinical experience of the interruption of a treatment. These patients who suddenly bring their treatment to an end have a paranoid disposition that is matched by a particular narcissistic vulnerability. It can be seen that their attempts to invest positively objects that prove resistant to self-projection are conflictualised or abandoned.

Moreover, recognised opportunities for instinctual drive activity (given the tendency towards the disunion of existing alloys) are feared, for they represent the danger that the ego's fluctuating boundaries will be breached to an intolerable extent.

Between the no-thing and nothing: the eroticisation of despair as a bond.

> "Your silence riddles me with its screams."
>
> (N., a patient)

If I have chosen to speak here about the case of Raphael, it is because for me he represented an extreme case of an analysis that is suddenly broken off, one that I had not anticipated in spite of the difficulties of the treatment.

Raphael, a refined-looking man in his sixties but who seemed younger, came to see me because, as he said to me, quoting Dante:

> "In the middle of the journey of our life I came to myself within a dark wood where the straight way was lost."
>
> (Dante, 1472)

The eldest of two siblings, Raphael had had little contact with his father who was constantly away for professional reasons. He had been brought up by his mother, a housewife, who attracted him to herself in order to discharge an excess of tension. However, not only was she unable to receive and transform the emotions she aroused in this way, but she was also prone to behaving violently. She had died shortly before the love affair that would lead him to undertake an analysis.

After immigrating to France, his professional career had developed very swiftly, to the point that he gained an international reputation. He was married to a woman with whom he was very much in love, but she had been ill for many years now. She had left him very much alone with his desire for loving and sexual exchanges, only sharing with him her violence or depression. These seemed to be the residue of a passion that, according to him, was the *raison d'être* of their coupledom. In fact, their relationship, it seemed, had been quite unhappy since the beginning, but this had been concealed by their outward social image. They have three young adult children.

He talked about his sense of duty and family loyalty to excuse his inability to separate from his wife, whom he none the less described as very unsatisfactory. In fact, he always returned to her in search of a verbal or silent violence, a torment which, it seems, eroticised despair as a bond between them.

He then met a brilliant woman with whom he had, he said, a "dream relationship", for she desired him and appreciated him for what he was; their exchanges enriched his thought and helped him to rediscover the strength of his desire: he began once again to have erotic dreams.

At the heart of this constellation, Raphael gave the impression that he was experiencing a deep change in his sense of self, of his body, and of his perception of the world: this took the form of a hypercathexis of the imaginary world, a refusal of the demands of external reality, an overestimation of himself and a close dependence on the loved object, all of which resulted in both a shrinking of the relational and perceptual field and an invasion of his mind by the representation of the person he loved. This description evoked the similarity between the state of being in love and a primitive state of the psyche in which the self is the centre of everything, comparable to the connection Freud (1917e, p. 244) establishes between the work of mourning and the state of being in love, between object-choice and narcissism. I could sense a desire in Raphael for total unification, for abolishing difference and distance.

However, this relationship quickly turned into a nightmare, repeating his marital experience: the same absence of coherence, the same separation and/or intrusion anxieties, the same fears of the beginnings of an implosion leading to an archipelago-type state of the ego that seemed to me to be closer to disintegration (due to the weakening of the container) than to fragmentation. Whereas the latter is the result of severe and active splitting of the ego in which denial is accompanied by a fantasy of annihilation, an archipelago-type state results from the erasure of the osmotic boundaries of the ego with the id and the superego so as not to overwhelm the psyche with excess excitation.

So, his dream foundered once again, owing to his denial of the share of reality that this new life experience contained. The apparent equilibrium was shattered. The demands linked to love and passion had become necessary companions. These attempts functioned like sound boxes in which the emotional charge was multiplied. Faced with intolerable experiences, Raphael was searching for a rational explanation, perhaps reassurance or support, to help him survive a passionate love affair that had its roots in the opacity of his refusal to recognise the truth about himself.

To protect himself against this depersonalising weakness, he adopted a drastic defence: in a movement of total detachment, he no longer felt he existed, either for himself or for others. In his outer life, he felt exploited by the external object who required him to make her happy. It was an impossible task if he wanted to maintain his past, but now vacillating, illusion of having an existence of his own. His inability to appropriate this dream relationship was expressed by an emotional disaffection and an inability to be present for his girlfriend: he would have run the risk of losing his illusion of identity in it.

In the analytic relationship, he nourished his blindness to the authentic beauty of his new relationship by regressing to the fantasy of being his mother's sole object of desire. This expression of a fundamental void due to his incomprehension regarding his mother's intentions was perceived so vividly by the analyst that her capacity to think was affected by it. The conflictual impact of the external beauty of the object apprehended sensually faced Raphael with the enigma of his interiority and, as Meltzer (1988, p. 22) puts it, he no longer knew if she was his Beatrice or his Belle Dame Sans Merci. His flight from the pain triggered by this conflict underlined his refusal to accept the separation–individuation—and, thus, the freedom—of the object, and dragged their relationship into an inevitable impasse.

Raphael wanted to start an analysis without delay, with very frequent sessions to ward off the pain aroused by the definitive break-up with his girlfriend.

After an early quasi-honeymoon period, and once the analyst–analysand pair were associated in creative and meaningful work together, I noticed that there was something in him that was jealous and envious of our capacities to think together: he then excluded himself from this process and demanded to have the setting that we had established all for himself—a setting that not only gave him the impression that time had been suspended but also the illusion of being in an atmosphere and place that were already familiar to him, a pleasure that was deliciously troubling. After a few weeks, he had a dream in which he felt he was floating in a pale green environment. Associating it with his experience of the atmosphere of the sessions, he said to me, "Here, silence reigns, the lights are dimmed, your voice reaches me from a felted distance, and me, I am floating on the couch as if in an aquarium."

This state constituted a reunion with archaic oneness, the primacy of the imaginary realm, a fusional experience of plenitude and of the state of being in love. It was at this moment, faced with such an imperious desire for my presence, that I experienced a movement of withdrawal in my countertransference.

I understood that this pressure from Raphael, stemming from his logic of the pleasure principle and his feeling of omnipotence, was making me feel intruded upon. My countertransference response was to withdraw narcissistically, rather than being containing, in order to protect the object that I was experiencing as seductive. The more I withdrew, the more Raphael was intrusive. By seeking to reanimate the object-relation that was becoming more and more absent, his avidity was generating a masochistic experience for which he held me responsible.

I had offered to see him three times a week initially, and then four times as soon as I could, but I sensed quite quickly that he experienced this response as both excessive and insufficient.

A triangular situation thus appeared, paradoxically without a third party. The meaning and thought that emerged from our meetings were squeezed out by his suffering, which annihilated the fruit of our associated reveries. Raphael recovered them through a movement of narcissistic compliance, while refusing to acknowledge the value of the discovery of their significance. And I noticed that this would not have occurred without my participation. The more he made attacks on linking, the more my hostility became manifest in my thoughts.

Surreptitiously, I felt an archaic suffering surfacing in me as well, which was all the more unthinkable in that it was at the origin of the process of thinking itself.

Raphael had turned me into an object that was never there, but, at the same time, a source of torments and, thus, intrusive, pulling him towards nothingness. Because he wavered constantly between two opposing excesses, gratification on the one hand and frustration on the other, his excitation prevented any activity of linking.

We were both subjected to an increasingly strong state of passivation due to his attacks on the feminine and maternal dimensions in me. The relationship took on a sadomasochistic colouring and brought to light a repudiation of psychic femininity; this, in turn, led us to an erasure of the mother's love for the father and for the child, which found expression in Raphael's need to be the mother's sole object, thereby filling with terrifying emotions the space from which thinking might eventually have emerged.

He was once again overwhelmed by drive excitation (the germs of madness internally), which could have been contained if the source of the drive of the object, secreted in the relationship, had not created a second, external, defensive front against them. So, instead of being his ally, I was becoming his enemy (like the internal object), leading him to attack both the object and me, rendering the alpha function inoperative (Bion, 1992, p. 216).

In this universe, Raphael felt lost and became incapable of distinguishing his own impulses from those of the object. He then panicked and, in a state of complete confusion, faced with both separation and intrusion anxiety, reacted by isolating himself. To say the least, he preserved an incommunicable zone that was projected on to my silence, which he experienced at moments not as listening, but as a silence of death. The analysis unfolded within the context of a relationship that oscillated between disconnected communication, the zero of silence, and my growing frustration.

Bion has stressed the importance of two forms of hatred: that of the external world and that of the internal world. Raphael's attacks on linking sought to struggle against quantities of affect that were in danger of submerging his psychical organisation.

If separation implies a shared contract, and if the analytic contract requires this separation to be elaborated (as in any relationship), it is also a link that involves a third party. So, Raphael attacked the setting and, through the ambiguity of his discourse, my capacity to make links. If one thinks of the setting as the space of resonance and signification which enables one both to hear what comes up and to bring into existence what one hears, the plurality of the links gives flesh to speech.

If the possibility of escaping the primitive madness of the object is the function of the father, Raphael's father, who had been absent and experienced as envious of the mother–son relationship, was neither a mediator, because he did not contain the mother's anxieties, nor the object of her sexual drives. He offloaded these tasks on to his son who, as a result, imagined that, as he was the eldest son, he was the sole object of his mother's love.

By being active, the drive rendered him passive, and I became a mother who was making him undergo the torment of Tantalus, for all Raphael could do was to try to decipher her desire and understand the place that it occupied for her, which created mutual incomprehension and misunderstanding. He felt more and more excluded from the thinking couple that we formed, and rebelled against each separation imposed by the setting, such as weekends or holidays, moments when, in the grip of emotions that he was unable to contain, he multiplied the means of controlling the "never present" object and violently attacked the analytic pair itself. Moreover, he bitterly denounced the one-sided character of the rules of the setting when he had to pay for his missed sessions.

Now the analytic treatment and relationship were only possible through a trusting passivation in which Raphael would put himself in the analyst's hands. Freud (1937c, p. 250) noted that, for both sexes, the repudiation of femininity constitutes a bedrock standing in the way of cure. But, as Green (1986, p. 252) writes, it is more a question of repudiating the mother's femininity, that is to say, her passivating effect.

If Eros constitutes linking, hatred, for its part, is an attack that also includes a positive aspect: it creates a discontinuity without which new links could not be established, for a state of continuum would be an unlimited fusional space. In the transference–countertransference relationship, what we found ourselves faced with was the erotisation of the passivity and despair of this passion. This is the meaning that emerges from every separation introduced by a third party and which reweaves the contact barrier punctured by the attacks on/discontinuity of, linking, permitting the object and creativity of triangulation to be rediscovered. Without passion between a man and a woman, the passion between mother and child is vitiated. The state of love gives rise to a sense of revenge on the parental couple, serving to repair the experience of being evicted from the adult sexual world. It provides the superego with reassurance through gratifying love. All the ingredients are there to seal the initial massively narcissistic character of love. The discovery of the love-object is a rediscovery and reconstitution.

If one compares the paintings representing the Virgin and Child and those depicting the Passion of the Son, it is noticeable that they all contain murmurs of the death of the son and the still unanswered question: "Father, why have you forsaken me?"

The passion for the father is not secondary, but different. There are differences between passions, just as there differences between the sexes.

The limits of the setting put the relationship in a state of tension, and it was, thus, necessary to restructure the identity of the analyst–analysand couple threatened by the intensity of the exchanges. Raphael's drive impulses breached his ego, causing narcissistic anxieties against the intrusion of the internal object, which he thought he had got rid of by withdrawing into himself, with the help of sublimation, but this defence was undermined by the passionate relationship.

Thus, sexuality and aggressiveness were combined in a violence that was imposed from the inside, reflecting the violence of the internal object which prohibited acceptance of the alterity of thought itself. I detected in Raphael the existence of a subtle way of thinking which was careful not to reveal his thoughts to an object/analyst for fear that she might intuit the existence of a quasi-symbiotic relationship. His defence against the supposed intrusive avidity that sought to possess and control the object was manifested, on the contrary, by a withdrawal into "his" way of thinking. Any interpretation in terms of projective identification met with violent resistance on his part, for it would have implied that he agreed that the movement began in him, whereas, in fact, he always claimed that the violence came from outside.

He constantly resorted to a reversal of perspectives. All initiatives had their source in external reality. The countertransferential movements to which I sometimes yielded, out of a need to relieve my psychical apparatus, were a confirmation for him of the need to consolidate his narcissistic defences against a hostile alterity. Our relationship became paradoxical, thus radically disturbing, overflowing with anxiety and insecure.

His associations were so disconnected that, for me, they suggested images without links between them, as if he was refusing the analyst's mediation with a view to clarifying the situation. For example, he said to me, "A meeting with colleagues. This weekend, I am going skiing. I also had lunch with my daughter yesterday. But this evening, I am going to the opera with my wife." Protected by this wall of language that was difficult to decipher, his thoughts were less the fulfilment of a wish than a repudiation of any form of alterity. Our apparently fusional relationship was, thus, a means for him to keep his thoughts out of reach. For Raphael, thinking did not consist in linking processes, but rather in linking them up again secretly after disconnecting them.

When he would say to me, "Say something to me", he was making sure that he had not lost his inviolable refuge and, paradoxically, that he had proof, at any given moment, of the other's existence: by requiring me to do the talking, he avoided having to reveal himself. It was these feelings of jealousy, fury, and rivalry that had led him to sever the link in order to preserve an object that he had never possessed—and, therefore, never lost—whose destiny was to protect him against any possibility of meeting or losing the loving object.

Indeed, it was when I had to modify the setting by deferring a few sessions for unforeseen reasons, that he decided to break off the treatment, for he could not bear not having total control of the situation himself. In this way, in a final manifestation of his power over me, he kept me paradoxically at a distance from a third party that excluded him and which, consequently, he himself attacked. Breaking off the treatment was the expression of a "never without you"/"never with you": in other words, breaking off the treatment could also be a way of keeping the analyst.

In a dream, Raphael saw a "Cetacea" (*cétacé*) (and I understood "*c'est assez*" (that's enough)), without limbs, stranded on a beach like a mammal ejected from its oceanic environment. This vision was evocative for me of his twofold impossibility of advancing and of forming One with the mother (*mère*) (*mer* = sea): an enormous aborted foetus.

At this point, a long-buried impulse of protest was suddenly amplified, and his decision to break off the treatment, which was acted out through his sudden departure, came as a hammer blow. Was it an act of retaliation for the tantalising nature of the analytic technique that had become unbearable? If one accepts that the time of analysis is unconsciously equated with the living body of the mother, the decision to break off the analysis then assumes the symbolic meaning of a veritable matricide.

The deferment of sessions reactivated the effects of an earlier trauma, allowing a violence that had hitherto remained hidden to emerge. Owing to the frustration inherent to the analytic situation and the fear aroused by the process itself, this violence had reached an intolerable level, akin to a catastrophic experience. His compelling need for my presence manifested this perfect unity between the subject's identity and the breast. The intrauterine relationship, where the absence of absence reigns, may be considered as archetypal, for absence is a potential presence which makes linking or relating possible. His intolerable sensation of being torn apart at each separation originated partly in the terribly painful experience of early separation.

To conclude

It is true that analyses that are broken off suddenly can be seen in general as deferred effects of early traumatisms, the retroactive emergence of a certain violence that is inherent to the analytic situation but which has reached degree of subjective intensity that is intolerable. In certain cases, it is ineluctable, whether the analyst has sensed it or not. The boundaries of the analytic setting are sometimes a source of suffering and bitterness which are all the more acute because they follow the fleeting satisfactions of a nostalgia that is exacerbated by the dynamism of associative work but, at the same time, is sufficient to itself; or, alternatively, because they follow a sense of shared closeness found in a fruitful exchange or in a reparative silence which blurs the sharp edges of individuality, thereby attenuating the dissymmetry of the situation.

It is understandable, in certain transference situations, when a sense of closeness is too marked or too sudden, that breaking off the treatment represents the sole means of escaping anxiety that is uncontainable. Without it being a question of important interpretations, even simple interventions, or just the manifestation of the analyst as distinct and separate, sometimes are sufficient to trigger a reaction of rejection, as if it were a case of an intolerable graft. A fierce and proud will for autonomy hardens into a demand for autarchy, which, incidentally, is unrealisable.

To continue the analysis would be to suffer a defeat. To collaborate with the analytic work would be to expose the patient, inevitably, to "being had" sooner or later. A dread of passivity, a refusal of femininity, an intolerance of psychic bisexuality, and an impossibility of mourning infantile omnipotence, all underlie this negativism. One sometimes has the impression that one has come up against a schizoid bastion that has long remained imperceptible, hidden behind a relational transaction that is quite supple and an apparent permeability of the capacity for identification. Splitting is always present. Now, the aim of psychoanalysis in such a case, with the transference as a lever, consists in trying to create bridges between the parts that are split off from each other, that is, "anastomoses", if I may put it like that, between the contradictory dispositions: in short, to achieve very gradually a relative unification of this fragmented structure. Such an attempt risks inducing a solution of flight through acting out, through the symbolically murderous violence of breaking off the analysis, the only appropriate solution in the eyes of the patient who feels he is faced with the danger of being crushed narcissistically. Cutting the time of analysis is a way of externalising the splitting and perhaps of trying to reproduce cathartically the violent separation of birth.

Being subjected to such a heavy burden in the transference passion is extenuating. The countertransference is in the front line here. Such patients open us up to the logic of despair: reduced to touching nothing but the wind when each word maintains the illusion of contact, they then sense the absurdity of this gesture towards the other which cannot pierce the night as long as space is an enemy for them.

Note

1. Translated by Andrew Weller.

References

Bion, W. R. (1967). Attacks on linking. In: *Second Thoughts* (pp. 93–109). London: William Heinemann.

Bion, W. R. (1992). *Cogitations*. London: Karnac.

Dante, A. (1472). *The Divine Comedy*. New York: Oxford University.

De La Vergne, G. J. (1669). *The Letters of a Portuguese Nun*. Charleston: Nabu.

Freud, S. (1912d). On the universal tendency to debasement in the sphere of love. *S. E., 11*: 179–190. London: Hogarth.

Freud, S. (1917e). Mourning and melancholia. *S. E., 14*: 243–258. London: Hogarth.

Freud, S. (1937c). Analysis terminable and interminable. *S. E., 23*: 216–253. London: Hogarth.

Freud, S. (1940a). *An Outline of Psychoanalysis. S. E., 23*: 144–207. London: Hogarth.

Green, A. (1986). Passions and their vicissitudes. In: *On Private Madness* (pp. 214–253). London: Hogarth.

Klein, M. (1986)[1946]. Notes on some schizoid mechanisms. In: *Envy and Gratitude* (pp. 1–24). London: Virago.

Meltzer, D. (1988). The aesthetic conflict: its place in the developmental process. In: D. Meltzer & M. H. Williams (Eds.), *The Apprehension of Beauty: The Role of Aesthetic Conflict in Development, Art and Violence* (pp. 7–31). London: Karnac.

CHAPTER EIGHT

Escaping to Frankenstein

Edna O'Shaughnessy

The paper "Attacks on linking" concludes Bion's series in the 1950s on the psychotic personality and its schizoid mechanisms. Based on Freud and Klein, his series, together with the work of Rosenfeld (1965) and Segal (1957) brought to psychoanalysis a new understanding of psychosis. I shall be trying to think again about the analysis of a young patient of mine in the light of Bion's "Attacks on linking" (Bion, 1959), the nature of the transference and the outcome of the analysis, his need to express himself by the use of what I shall call "ready-mades", and the pivotal moment in the analysis when he turned away from the analyst to Frankenstein.

This is a return to a patient I have written about before, a boy of twelve, Hugh, as I call him, with a psychosis who came mentally broken down and who, after three years of analysis, left able to resume his life and his education, while at the same time keeping an intense relationship with Frankenstein.

As told to me by his parents, Hugh was born at a time when his mother was very stressed by having to cope with too much—illness in the family and the running of a too-large house. It was their housekeeper who told them, after six weeks, that their new baby screamed all the time because he was hungry. Hugh was given a bottle to supplement breastfeeding but he still screamed. Later, he disliked, and was not able to work in, a succession of schools. His education finally stopped when his father fetched him home, broken down and weeping, from his weekly boarding school.

Since then Hugh had lived at home, unable to be alone, go out, or let his parents go out together He filled his room with all kinds of rubbish, broken things and bits he picked up everywhere—Hugh's "habits", they called it. No one was allowed into his room to sort or clean. "He rules the household." Father and mother were angry with Hugh, especially mother, who looked very grim and depressed. More recently, they had become alarmed that Hugh was becoming dangerous—he had started lighting fires that nearly got out of control in the long grass at the bottom of the garden. Yet, as well, Hugh's parents were much concerned, and were trying to be honest.

Here is my description of Hugh's first session.

> Father brought Hugh to the first session. I saw a beautiful boy, with a nice smile, rigid and sad, clinging to father. In the playroom, Hugh was terrified and stayed standing, clinging to a small chair. He gazed out of the window and looked, not at me or the furnishings, but at the spaces between. From his hovering gaze, I could tell that these spaces seemed to him to be full of particles.
>
> Hugh was in a state of high psychotic arousal. I spoke to him about what he was letting me know: his terror, the bits around him everywhere, his need to hold on to the chair for safety. He was trying to suck the point of his shirt collar. I said he was wanting something like a breast here—a mistake I discuss later. As time went on, there were other events. Hugh looked at the open drawer of playthings, at first with curiosity, then contempt, and then, I thought, in fear of my contempt if he were interested. Unspontaneously, only in response to a question from me, he spoke a few words in a dead tone, rubbing his finger and thumb together.
>
> To his second session, Hugh arrived with two books and a newspaper. This was the start of his characteristic way of communicating with what I shall call "ready-mades". He placed the book so I could see it was called *More about Paddington.* On the cover was a colourful picture of a cute little bear sitting on a chair with a cushion. Hugh lived in the country and travelled by train to Paddington Station to come to his sessions. I understood, as I said to him, that he was offering me a picture of himself and his new analysis. He was the little bear, the analysis was a cushion

> for him—a place for him to be—and he wanted more. Meanwhile, he was staring anxiously at the wall and rubbing his belt. Eventually, he was able to tell me he was watching a hand pointing a finger. He moved the book aside to reveal a headline on the newspaper: "BOY FRIEND, EXTRA". I interpreted he felt very afraid of, and pointed at, by the hand, accused of masturbation, and wanted me to know his penis was an extra, like a boyfriend to hold on to in a frightening world.

In these early sessions, Hugh was in a space of evacuated small particles and big looming things like the hand pointing a finger he saw in a shadow on the wall—a bizarre object in Bion's sense. A second alarming presence evacuated from his mind was a watching eye he saw on the latch of the window. The little chair he held on to, like his penis, his father, and, I think, also myself, signified things in the real world that stopped him from being overwhelmed by psychotic panic in a menacing space with two hostile presences and fragments and bits. Even while terrified, Hugh could let me know he was grateful for the relief he gained from having his terror and the nature of his threatening world recognised. He often made an affirmatory "Mmmm" sound and continued to communicate with occasional speech, body movements, and pictures and newspaper headlines that he brought to the sessions.

As his anxiety subsided and his need for schizoid mechanisms to evacuate his terrified mind lessened, his experience of the room as full of bits disappeared . He became able to sit down at the table. First, he played a little perfunctorily with toys and paper. Then he started to draw. His drawings were not of people, but of shapes in black and white (never colour), showing me in this way his world of bleak part-objects .

The first time Hugh made a drawing, as is usual I asked him, for our work, to keep it in his drawer. He complied. However, when the patient who came after him left, I found Hugh outside my front door, distressed and weeping. He said he could not go without his drawing. I realised then that leaving his drawing, for him, would be a mutilation of his self and I fetched it for him to take home, which, from then on, he always did.

I already knew that drawing made Hugh anxious about bits of himself leaking out on the page. The activity of drawing also opened his anus, and he would become alarmed at the unstoppable smells coming out of his bottom and worried also that his drawing was leaking through the paper, frequently turning it over to check its underside. These were Hugh's relations to his objects—primitive and concrete uncontainedness in himself, likewise in his objects, in the uninvited presence of a hostile spoiling force like the smells from his bottom. He often drew bits, pieces, vague trails of shapes. I came to know, what he already knew, how he felt in danger of bits of his self and his objects seeping out, in breath, or speech, or from his fingers when he drew, and getting lost in the paper or the room. To prevent these losses, he held himself rigidly, was sparing of movement and words. In addition, in attempts to recover what he had lost, if he saw "a bit"—even a bit of fluff or speck of dirt—he picked it up and put it in his pocket, saying tonelessly, "One of my habits", doing in his sessions, as I knew from his parents, what he did at home—compulsively collecting all kinds of bits and pieces for storage in his room.

It was the emergence in the analysis of "a psychological disaster", as Bion calls it (1967b, p. 83), still active and without resolution—the mental state of the hungry, screaming baby Hugh once was, who, even when well fed with a bottle, still screamed, unable to recover. In his first session, when he tried to suck the point of his collar and I interpreted his wanting to find something like a breast to suck, I had failed to understand that Hugh was beyond hunger and the need for a feeding breast and in a condition of terror of losing what was left of life within himself, even as he also felt threatened with annihilation by hostile external objects. Trying to suck his collar, I then realised, was a search for a plug to prevent his self from pouring away through his mouth.

Another symptom of Hugh's illness was symbolic impairment. Rather than being symbols, his words often, though not always, were symbolic equations in Segal's sense: the symbol is equivalent to the object and so the thinking is concrete (Segal, 1957). Hume has recently explored the communication problems, for analyst and patient, of a patient with a fragmented ego (Hume, 2016). It is interesting to note how close Bion's notion of the destructive attacks on the function of linking is to Freud's description of the workings of the death instinct. Freud writes, "beside the instinct [Eros] to preserve living substance and to join it into ever larger units, there must exist *another, contrary instinct seeking to dissolve those units . . .*" (1930a, p. 118, original emphasis). I think it is the dissolution of units, the attacks on linking, *viz.*,

Hugh's enormous need in his abnormal early development for excess use of schizoid mechanisms of defence that destroyed the vitality of a large part of his mind and left his language in a sterile state—two ideas do not engender a third, there are few paths of association, and the range of reference of his words is restricted. We might think of it as "death in the mind" making his language of little use for new or complex notions—one reason for Hugh's need for "ready-mades" to express himself, and because ready-mades are not his, little psychic work, for which Hugh has only limited capacity, is required and he can communicate without fear of loss of his self.

I think Hugh came to his second session afraid I would not want "more" of the manifestly psychotic youth of the day before and felt he must win me over. But all his handicaps meant he himself could not be "winsome" and needed the help of a "ready-made" like Paddington Bear.

I am borrowing the term "ready-made" from the surrealist Marcel Duchamp. Marcel Duchamp's "ready-mades" were ordinary manufactured objects he offered as art in opposition to what he called "retinal art" (Cabanne, 1971). Breton emphasised the lack of individuality of ready-mades. Being neither "retinal" nor "individual" applies also to Hugh's ready-mades, albeit with a different source and purpose. The surrealists wished to provoke and question, and offered their works with humour and irony. Hugh's use of ready-mades—pictures, stories, newspaper headlines—that he brought to his sessions came not only from his symbolic impairment, but also from his anxieties about contact: with himself and with his hostile internal and external objects, and from his terror of the loss of self through communications. On first arriving, Hugh, too, had a brief retinal image: he looked at me with one eye which then sort of "took me" in the way a camera does, with a peculiar movement that seemed to slice off the front of me. Then he was *in* a world with the hostile watching eye on the window and the finger pointing at him from the wall, but protected also by the "cushion" of the analysis. I think it was to himself, to me, and to these watching, condemning objects that he offered the winsome picture of Paddington Bear, a picture so very different from the reality of the terrified psychotic youth of his first session.

Hugh began to carry with him everywhere a book called *A Creepy World* inside a transparent bag. I understood this as a concrete representation of his omnipotent phantasy (for him, not a phantasy but a fact) of having crept into analysis with a bag always around him. For Hugh, I was not a person, but a series of part-objects: the bag around him, some function such as power, attention, or understanding, and I was uncertainly safe. He was always anxious about attack: any small noise or movement made him rigid with fear. In some sessions when this world turned threatening, with finger movements, or the flicker of an eye muscle, or the grinding of a top tooth on a bottom tooth, Hugh attacked these enemies. Even so, I was hugely, if ambiguously, significant to him.

The phantasy, for Hugh not a phantasy but a fact, that he was all the time inside a transparent bag lasted until the session when I told him about the first holiday break of the analysis. He swung round and stared at me, his face wide in shocked disbelief. The next day, he came with a drawing of misaligned concentric circles with a sunken gap. Fired by outrage, he was suddenly verbal. He said accusingly, "England and France were once joined. Then a volcano came and they got separated. The middle bit got sunk and now its like this", pointing to the misalignments, the sunken bit, and the gap. I said he was showing me what I had done to him. He no longer felt whether we were near or far, that we were joined and I was around him. Now we were mismatched, and he felt sunk in his middle. Hugh drew a moon with four (he had four sessions) rockets round it which he said dropped darts of air on the moon and then there would be enough air to live. As he drew he made smell after smell, and got frantic because he could not stop. Next, he drew an earth and a distant moon with craters which the four rockets were leaving. These pictures told of the life-giving quality of his four sessions and how, in the analytic break, he felt left far away with a dead moon with black holes and no air to stay alive. Hugh responded to my first absence with elemental intensity. The shock of my absence left him sunk and angry, his orifices open and incontinent; he accuses me of failing to match his need of me to be always round him for life's sake, and he is left marked by the craters of my violence.

During this first break, Hugh's beauty vanished. He returned with sores and pimples round his mouth, a cut on his thumb, dirty and dim looking like a too-long-neglected infant. With trembling hands, he took from his drawer a paintbox he had never touched before, drew it from its wrappings, and opened it to gaze at the colours. He grew calm. I spoke to him about how, alone in the break, he felt life had gone, but now when he saw the colours were still here, it meant: there is *life* here that I kept for him.

But life had changed. Instead of his *Creepy World* book in a transparent bag, Hugh now carried with him a flicker booklet. By flicking its pages he made a "film" of a figure jumping up from one end of a seesaw so that the figure on the other end was shot into space. He often anxiously halted the film with a figure stranded in mid-air to picture his dread that at any moment I might get up and go, and hurtle him out. On this seesaw, if I was up, he was down, and *vice versa,* so showing me a central axis of our relations. He could, and did, reverse our places, and make me know and endure his paranoid position by keeping me unwanted, stranded in his silence in horrific dead hours. Hugh brought a cloth cap with a "popper" on its "flap" and pressed the popper in and out, to show me his repeated attempts to pop into objects to escape his "flap", that is, his anxieties, but his objects keep pushing him out. Rosenfeld (1965) emphasises how central intrusion into—as opposed to relating to—the object is to psychotic object relations. In this hostile, battling world, very much now the situation with his parents, who were trying to get Hugh moving out of the house, he showed me his methods of entry and control. He made paper squirrels and frogs with extended tails and tongues, and drew eyes on stalks. Specific omnipotent phantasies emerged about how the flatus from his tail, or his spittle, or his tongue, indeed any organ or body product, could dart out to bridge the gap between himself and object, enter it, and control it. Hugh was excited and very admiring of these "opposite of the ordinary" ways, as he called them, his secret entries into his objects, even as they made an eerie world with invisible threads and wires connecting him to objects who, in their turn, might try to enter and control him. His contemptuous refusal even to try "ordinary" ways was another source of his parents' resentment.

During this time, he often brought two boomerangs. He threw them at the wall, saying despondently and self-pityingly, "They never go anywhere, they don't come back to me", showing me how what he threw out, his communications, are not received or responded to. He conveyed intense despair, still feeling in himself the neglected baby, now a youth, whose parents (as I could currently observe for myself) did not comprehend the enormity of his illness, distress, and anxiety. Hugh represented his parents by swastikas in circles and as devils with horns. These they were not; these were Hugh's paranoid distortions of them as totally bad and hostile. In analysis, in the same way, he cut off our moments of good contact and retreated into self-pity for my failings and the shocks (especially the break) I gave him.

Even so, Hugh's psychotic functioning lessened. At home, he became able to stay by himself, at first for brief periods. Then he made expeditions on his own to his local town. In my notes of that time, I record that he was much less anxious and more alive. He started lessons again with a private tutor. His parents were enormously relieved. They soon insisted, in my view prematurely, that he make the journey to his sessions, by country bus, train to Paddington, then London underground to me, alone. Except for one or two days when they yielded to his entreaties to be brought by car, Hugh came on his own, sometimes suffering horrendous levels of fear, which his parents, persecuted by their bondage to him, but also recognising he needed pushing out, could not allow themselves to know.

When Hugh had been in analysis for a year, he made a declaration: "I can now see two-way traffic; last term in the road there was only one-way traffic. But now there are some road-works at the top of the hill." It was, in his own words, an acknowledgement of the two-way work between him and me. That evening his mother telephoned to complain that she was unbearably depressed, Hugh was impossible, she could not stand it. To the next session there came a different Hugh, cold and superior. "Why do I have to come? I don't find you do anything", he said loftily, after which he saw "bits of dirt shining in the sun"—the bits, I thought, of his appreciative self of the day before in dirty fragments, now pushed out of himself. Here was my first glimpse of the problems recognition of a helpful good object brings Hugh: depression (at once projected into his mother), and the hatred of an arrogant self who dissolves the link between him and a good object (cf. Segal's (1956) account of depression in the schizophrenic).

Nevertheless, a new era had begun. Over the next months there were sequences of acknowledged two-way endeavours between him and me, the most intense occurring when his parents went away for two weeks on their first holiday in years. Alone, Hugh made the long journeys to and from his sessions. He felt his parents had been torn out of him, leaving holes from which more and more of him was lost daily. He stood at the window watching leaves being blown by the wind and told me in a voice choked with fear that there was a tree without any leaves on it. This was his ultimate dread: he would fall to pieces, be dispersed like leaves in the wind, and cease to exist. By the end of the fortnight, he had dwindled to a standstill.

His crisis in his parents' absence repeats his traumatised reaction to the first analytic break, but with a difference: he now had an object to come to and afterwards he was movingly grateful. During the next weeks, our relations were more alive, even though, at the same time, he hated his dependence on me. He made a puppet of paper and string, and showed me how the strings went into the puppet, held its bits together, and pulled the puppet along and made it walk—a cruel and humiliating image that spoiled the good link between patient and analyst.

Even so, Hugh continued to progress. When he returned from the next analytic break, on the Monday he was very pleased to be back. He spoke about a Morse code buzzer with a missing part, of its needing to be picked up, wanting to send messages, and its being recharged when the two parts were fitted together, which I understood and interpreted as his experiences of the break and his pleasure that we were together again. But, by Thursday, he had changed—he was persecuted and sullen. He brought with him a toy he said was "a green man tied by strings to a parachute". Not looking at me, he told the story of Snow White, the Queen, the mirror, and the question: "Who is the fairest of them all?" He ended by stating that Snow White has dwarves who do all the work for her. I said he was telling a hateful story about us: I think I am Snow White, the "fairest of them all", and I am very pleased with myself though I do no work, but make him a dwarf who does all the work for me. While I was speaking, Hugh was dropping the green man on the table so that it pulled the parachute down, again and again. He said, "The green man is *too big* for the parachute." I spoke about how he wanted me to know that there is a green man in him who feels too big to have me as a parachute that holds him and helps him through the holiday and to return safely here—the green man cannot bear it, and is hating me with the Snow-White story.

It was to the next session that, for the first time, Hugh brought a large white mask and also a newspaper. He placed the mask on top of the newspaper saying, "It's a mask I made of Frankenstein; it's Frankenstein's monster, but I call it Frankenstein." With unusual feeling, he made a speech. "Frankenstein is human, not a robot. There", he indicated the wound with stitches drawn on the forehead, "he got hit with a chair when he went mad and broke the wires that held him. There should be a bolt" [he meant the bolt at the monster's neck] "but I did not put it in." He rubbed the back of the mask where there was an opening, saying, "I cut it down the back." Then he moved the mask aside to reveal an advertisement in the newspaper. It was a coloured picture of a young, uncomplicated, and pleasing woman in a white blouse against a blue sky, with the caption "LONDON PRIDE—BEAUTY IN BLOUSES", London Pride being the name of the firm making the blouses.

Hugh then turned his back on me. For the rest of the session, he busied himself with the Frankenstein mask. He spoke twice: he said he had made the mask from bits mixed with glue to make papier-mâché. He also said the monster is grey-green, hard and not soft. The professor made him from old things dug up from graves.

Hugh was in touch with reality—he knew it was a papier-mâché mask, and, at the same time, he felt he *was* the Professor who had assembled dead bits into a creature that was both his object and himself and whose work was above mine. As I was now beneath him, it lessened his Green Man hatred—he was only "grey-green". This axis of up and down was of central significance to Hugh, who veered between psychotic arrogance when up, and painful humiliation if down.

From then on Hugh brought the mask to almost every session, and ignored me and busied himself with Frankenstein. In terms of "Attacks on linking", it was an attack on the new live links developing between patient and analyst, and on the integrative links starting to occur within Hugh himself. It was also the emergence of Hugh's psychic predicament. On the day he first brought the mask, he had remarked that "There should be a bolt, but I did not put it in." I think the "bolt" he left out was his *bolt away* from feeling, for the first time, that he missed his analyst when she was not there, needed and depended on her as a good(ish) object. Hugh was bolting from the start of a depressive position he sensed was "too big", more than he could bear or we would safely manage, given how he and his objects are.

In his sessions, he now related Frankenstein's story, again and again, as if it were his story. He knew the story not from Mary Shelley's book *Frankenstein, or The Modern Prometheus* (1818), but from

James Whale's 1931 film in which Boris Karloff plays the monster. In the film, Frankenstein the scientist transgresses the limits of nature and makes a living creature from bits of criminals dug up from graves, and then rejects his monstrous creation. The appeal to Hugh of this story was very great. It expressed the truth of his deep sense of rejection by his objects and his painful awareness of being fragmented and different from other people. In her paper, "'Why am I here?'—selected aspects of the psychotic analysis of the boy" Wojciechowska (1997) describes a youth who was also drawn to Frankenstein. For Hugh, because Frankenstein is monstrous from rejection only, becoming Frankenstein was also an escape from his persecuting guilt and anxiety of being "a green man" whose narcissism means good relations so humiliate him that he hates and smashes them. Turning to Frankenstein was an escape into omnipotence, away from emotional pain and deprivation, and the anxiety that lost relations cannot be repaired and regained. Omnipotence is a feature of many "ready-made" projective identities: for example, God, Jesus, kings and queens, Napoleon.

Hugh spent his sessions elaborating elements of the Frankenstein tale. He would tell me how Frankenstein was not born, but built bigger than normal by science from old things dug up from graves, emphasising how *he* had made his papier-mâché monster from bits of old newspaper and glue. He was describing a Promethean act of self-creation, a transmuting of dead bits and pieces into a being whose birth and care were not owed to parents, and whose current better state was not owed to his analyst. On the mask, he often redrew the stitches of the wound "where Frankenstein got hit with a chair"—so recharging his grievance about separateness and separations.

There came a session when Hugh placed the mask in front of him on the table and looked at it with a leer of lascivious, excited anticipation. Then he put his head all the way into it and sat looking out at me from its eye slits. The atmosphere was eerie, mad, and frightening. There were many sessions like this. I thought he felt now it was *his* turn: just as a monster mother had got into his head, he was now inside the monster's head, seeing what it was like in there, and looking out and frightening me as he had been frightened as a small child, and, I believed, still was, within and without.

On television at this time there was a jokey series about fun monsters called *The Munsters*. Hugh started to wear the clothes of Frankenstein the Munster. He looked something like a jokey, eccentric teenager. He put his Frankenstein mask in a small suitcase, locked it, and carried it with him everywhere. He was now attending a "crammer" with larger groups of pupils and several teachers. He made a drawing of what he called "a framed picture of Frankenstein"—his only drawing in the analysis of a human figure. Frankenstein occupied all the picture. Outside the frame was a small pudgy face, about which he said contemptuously, "It is ordinary, it has a low forehead, it is not intelligent." He went on, "The monster has a high brow and is intelligent, and there is more of him." This mental state, in which Hugh unlinked himself from a despised "ordinary" self and instead was in a state of projective identification with Frankenstein, was never, except fleetingly, undone in the analysis.

I struggled with a patient who was hardly available. Hugh was "being Frankenstein" and engaging himself in working on and remodelling his papier-mâché mask. To his horror, there were times when the mask started to look more and more like his mother. Then he was frantic: he had not after all escaped into a new "ready-made" identity, but was still trapped with a pursuing, terrifying mother. Mostly, Hugh felt he *was* Frankenstein, his excitement escalated, and he grew alarmingly mad and manic, and sometimes dangerous. To my horror, he arrived one day and I could see a twelve-inch knife buckled to his belt. By this time he was a burly fourteen-year-old. I stopped him from going into our room, saying I was not sure I could keep us safe, or that he could, and I asked him to leave his knife in the waiting area. After a long and terrifying stand-off during which I was afraid he might try to enact a murderous phantasy, he unbuckled his knife and dropped it on the table. Then, in our room, he crawled along the floor to reach his drawer, communicating by action and projection as he did so the huge pain of an experience he felt not as his co-operation that made the session possible, but as utter humiliation.

I learnt from his parents that at home and school there were notable improvements, even though his "habits" of compulsively collecting bits, rubbish, newspapers, etc., to store in his room continued. Very hostile, Hugh brought to his sessions a gadget with a skinny hand that shot out to snatch away money, claiming this was what I was: a robber stealing money from his parents.

Rosenfeld (1964) in his paper "The psychopathology of narcissism", describes the primitive object relations of narcissism. He writes,

> In narcissistic object relations omnipotence plays a prominent part. The object ... is treated as the infant's possession ... into which are omnipotently projected the parts of the self which are felt to be undesirable as they cause pain or anxiety ... defences against any recognition of separateness between self and object play a predominant part ... separation would lead to feelings of dependence on an object and therefore to anxiety. Dependence implies love for, and recognition of the value of the object ... (pp. 170–171)

Here are some of the problems Hugh fears are "too big", irresolvable and dangerous, from which he seeks escape—not by means of psychic work with his own individual objects and his analyst, which he fears is "too big", but by means of a projective identification into a new ready-made and omnipotent identity, such as Frankenstein.

For the first time in his three years of analysis, Hugh began to nag his parents to stop. He found them willing allies. Enthusiastic about his improvement (he was now attending a "crammer" and coping with larger groups of children and several teachers) they felt all energies should be directed to placing him in a good school. Occasionally, his lost self returned in horror. He would say "Frankenstein is not real", or "Frankenstein is a kind of dead thing" and for a while he felt relieved. Then some distress or anxiety would drive him back to turning to and idealising Frankenstein, who brought him another sort of relief by giving him the feeling of having something protective around him that freed him from hatred, depression, and pain, and gave him the sense that all damage was fixable, plus excitement and energy at his triumph over me with this "opposite of the ordinary" solution by means of Frankenstein.

One day, unexpectedly, Hugh arrived in a quite different mood from his usual rigid, careful way. He came hurrying in with an affectionate grin, and handed me the newspaper he had brought, saying sadly, "An advertisement." It was "Beauty in Blouses". He conveyed acute sadness both in his tone of voice and also by projection. It was the second time he had brought the picture, the first being his "turning away" session when he put Frankenstein on top of Beauty in Blouses. I thought he was telling me he knew there was such a thing as "Beauty in Blouses" and also showing me how he might have been different if he had known "Beauty in Blouses", but that, for him, it remained an advertisement—a "might have been" which makes him feel very sad. I had not understood "Beauty in Blouses" in the session when I first saw it. I never felt I was "Beauty in Blouses" for Hugh, and, after an early mistake about his searching for a breast when he tried to suck his collar (discussed above), I had not again talked in terms of "breasts". I think on this day Hugh was able, briefly, to be in touch with an overwhelming feeling, a "too big" feeling, of harm done to himself, deprivation, and loss.

By the next day, he was again in earnest to bring the analysis down. He had taken a Judo course and made menacing karate cuts in the session, saying he could smash the table in half if he wanted. It was, in fact, a stout oak table he could not smash, which I think was important to him and represented his sense of having not been able to smash everything important to his despised "ordinary" self, including his analyst. Hugh was spoiling for a fight, waiting for me to challenge him. I thought anything I could say might push him into physical violence and I stayed silent.

From then on he met interpretations with loud shouts of "No", "Wrong", "Stupid". At home, he insisted he wanted no educational arrangements that would allow him to continue coming for analysis. His parents entered him in a school for the following academic year. At that moment, Hugh spoke of Judo tricks and a film in which a ruler was setting himself up as a god and that it was a bit mad to do that. This was a moment of fear that his parents and I were being ruled by his madness. They came to see me. I gave them my opinion that Hugh should continue his analysis. They acknowledged there was "some very odd behaviour indeed", but could not let themselves see more than that, and we agreed a date for termination.

As the end was approaching, very near to his last session, and using the same phrase "too big" he had used of the Green Man, Hugh said, "The rest is too big." A few days later, he related the only dreams of the analysis.

The three dreams

He said, "I had three dreams." In the first dream

> "I was emptying bits from my pockets and my mother was crying. I went up to her to put my arms around her . . ."

He stopped and started laughing. "Oh", he continued

> "and my mother turned round and said 'Don't worry; I am going to kill you'."

I said he was laughing only because his dream is so terrifying. He said dismissively, "It was scaring in the night" and continued, "I woke up and I must have turned round because I went to sleep with my blanket round me and my arm under it, and when I woke up [here his voice was throttled with anxiety] I was round the other way and my arm was out. I got out and ran away."

I asked if he knew why he went to his mother in the dream. He answered, "Because I was sorry." I then spoke to him about his deep unhappiness; he was sorry his habits upset his mother and he wanted her to know he was sorry. Yet, he is terrified of turning round and reaching towards her, because, as he saw her in his dream, she would not accept his sorry—the mother in his mind is murderously revengeful.

There was a long pause. Then Hugh said bleakly,

> "In the second dream you pursued me to my home and whichever way I ran, you caught me."

I spoke to him about how he was appealing to me to understand and to accept his wish to leave the analysis. He feels afraid I will force him to go where he does not want to and that I will try to take away the blanket around him that Frankenstein is for him.

After a pause, he said,

> "In the third dream there was a great hunt and I was with the great hunter. I was looking at a picture where guns were hidden."

This third dream is Hugh's tragic answer to the hunters in his inner world—he retreats from the depressive to the paranoid–schizoid position. We can now see more fully Hugh's plight. He has monstrous internal objects, a murderous superego, a relentless analyst, figures that are a mixture of reality plus his projections and destructiveness. Hugh functions with a preponderance of death instincts and keeps few benign experiences, for example, he deadens even the small event of an analyst recognising he laughs from terror when he tells his dream of the murderous mother. His destructive narcissism is at variance with his unlimited dependence, any frustration humiliates him intolerably. Further growth, Hugh fears, could threaten him with a paranoid or depressive breakdown, and there are hidden guns—might even lead to murder or suicide.

Yet, there is also a different "might have been" had there not been, in Bion's words, Hugh's "early psychological disaster". Hugh's ego is divided: there is his ill and "opposite of the ordinary" self, the "monster" who mostly fills the picture. But, pushed aside, is "what might have been", an "ordinary" self who quietly used the analysis to recover from the breakdown in which he arrived; who can acknowledge the "two-way traffic" between us, who can use language to make a speech about the impact on him of the first analytic break, and plead with me to understand his turning away to Frankenstein as a human response, and who could also have true dream thoughts.

In one of his last sessions, Hugh said he had been thrown in Judo and hurt his foot. He talked of an old programme, *Top Cat*, the one where an alley cat saw an abandoned baby in a park. He said he was tired and had been working at his history last night. I thought the ending of analysis felt to him something like his history—he felt like an abandoned baby He rubbed his fingers backwards and forwards, saying, "Crooked, not straight", and spoke about vampires and werewolves. I said he was in pain about his analysis stopping. It seemed to prove I was crooked: how else could I abandon him?

Hugh could feel, and allow himself or me to know, such things only briefly. He still brought his Frankenstein mask with him locked in his little suitcase. To his last session, he also brought two books and laid them on the table. One was a Judo book with a cover of a Judo expert pulling his opponent down. The other was *Frankenstein's Revenge*. Such were the images through which we were pressured to see the end: he and I are opponents. I, the expert, pull him down, and he, Frankenstein, takes his revenge by leaving the analysis—all of which is to keep depression and the pains of loss and good-bye at a distance.

How shall we regard this outcome? Considered in the usual terms, the clinical result is a failure. Hugh is not able to be much in contact with himself or his analyst, tolerate frustration, face separateness and loss, or integrate the deep split in his ego. Internally, he still has a murderous superego and relentless pursuing objects, full with his projections of pride and narcissism; externally, he carries about with him a Frankenstein mask locked up in a little suitcase—an artefact always there for a needed escape by projective identification (Klein,

1946). He retreats from the depressive position. I take seriously Hugh's intuition that further development will be "too big", which I think means unmanageable without breakdown or perhaps even murder or suicide: after all, in his third dream, "Guns are hidden in the trees".

Bion suggests in relation to schizophrenic patients that we should not think in these usual terms, that the patient "may achieve his own form of adjustment to reality which may be no less worthy of the title of 'cure' because it is not the same kind as that which is achieved by less disordered patients" (Bion, 1967a, p. 34). I would not go so far as to use the word "cure" in regard to Hugh, but I think, in Bion's words, he achieved "his own form of adjustment", which is to say, he found a way of leading a life.

There were two subsequent communications from Hugh. He wrote a short letter to tell me he had passed his school exams. A few years after that, he sent me a coloured postcard. On one side was a peacock, fanning a tail with myriad eyes. On the other side, Hugh wrote to say he had finished his course of study and obtained his diploma.

References

Bion, W. R. (1967a). Notes on the theory of schizophrenia. In: *Second Thoughts* (pp. 23–35). London: Heinemann.

Bion, W. R. (1967b). On arrogance. In: *Second Thoughts* (pp. 86–92). London: Heinemann.

Bion, W. R. (1967c). Attacks on linking. In: *Second Thoughts* (pp. 93–109). London: Heinemann.

Cabanne, P. (1971). *Dialogues with Marcel Duchamp*. London: Thames & Hudson.

Freud, S. (1930a). *Civilisation and its Discontents*, *S. E.*, *21*: 59–145. London: Hogarth.

Hume, F. (2016). Free association and some of its pretenders. *Bulletin of BPAS*, *52*(1): 2–10.

Klein, M. (1946). Notes on some schizoid mechanisms. *International Journal of Psychoanalysis*, *27*: 99–110.

Rosenfeld, H. (1964). On the psychopathology of narcissism: a clinical approach. *International Journal of Psychoanalysis*, *45*: 332–337.

Rosenfeld, H. (1965). *Psychotic States*. London: Hogarth.

Segal, H. (1956). Depression in the schizophrenic. *International Journal of Psychoanalysis, 37*: 339–343.

Segal, H. (1957). Notes on symbol formation. *International Journal of Psychoanalysis, 38*: 391–397.

Shelley, M. (1818). *Frankenstein*. London: Lackington, Hughes, Harding, Mavor, & Jones [Penguin edition, 1985, repr. 1992, revised 2003].

Wojciechowska, E. (1997). "Why am I here?" – selected aspects of the psychotic analysis of the boy. *World of Psychoanalysis, 1-2*.

CHAPTER NINE

Attacks on linking, or uncontainability of beta elements?

Antonino Ferro

In the brief commentary that prefaces the Italian edition of "Attacks on linking", Bordi (1970) calls this work one of the greatest contributions to the expansion of Klein's thought, and emphasises how it is thanks to this paper that the concept of envy of the breast finds a place in the dialectic of the instincts.

Furthermore, in Bordi's opinion, Bion's paper gives the same weight to the features acquired during development as it does to those linked to the internal world and the instincts. In addition, it distinguishes those internal objects that belong to the ego from those that are delegated to the superego. I would now like to make a close and systematic examination of the work's theoretical aspects.

95

An interesting early observation concerns the assertion made by Bion at the IPA Congress of 1957 that the analogy between psychoanalytic and archaeological research had meaning only if addressed to the examination "not so much of a primitive civilization, as of a primitive catastrophe", and, indeed, his claim that the catastrophe we are seeking shifts in the very moment at which we study it is evidence of his divergence from Freud, who thought in terms of a leisurely examination, and also from Winnicott (1974) who, in his famous "Fear of breakdown", wrote of a breakdown that has already happened.

Bion goes further and establishes *ante litteram* the concept of the "analytic field", in whose presentness all the events of the analysis occur. Indeed, it gives us pause for thought that, without theorising it, Bion frequently uses the term "analytic field" in this work, and this is no cooled deposit of lava, but fluid, flaming lava, constantly appearing just below the surface of the field. The phenomena of eruption and evacuation are occurring in the very moment of our search. One of the destructions caused by this proto-emotional magma, full of consequences, is that of curiosity, the absence of which will prevent learning.

Another very useful way in which Bion clarifies matters is that he puts us on guard against considering a part-object as if it had an anatomical structure "because the part-object relationship is not with the anatomical structures only but with function, not with anatomy but with physiology, not with the breast but with feeding, poisoning, loving, hating" (p. 102). It would be difficult not to see in these observations, expressed in terms of alpha function, the germ of a concept that will be catastrophic for all preceding models of the mind.

In the face of the catastrophe, we cannot ask ourselves "Why did it happen?" but only "In what does it consist?"

96

It is at this point that Bion gives a wonderful description of what, when better organised, will become his model of the mind and will shift the interest of analysis away from contents to "tools for thinking dreaming feeling" (Ferro, 2015). He treats projective identification as a normal mode of functioning, one that is able to create a link between analyst and patient or infant and breast. There are analyses in which projective identification becomes the principal mode of communication, whether because the patient has not sufficiently developed from this modality, or because the analytic situation itself gives the opportunity for this modality to develop. Here, Bion has a stroke of genius which will open up his strongly relational theoretical model, the "better connected patient" and "without memory and desire": the patient sometimes "felt there was some object that denied him the use of projective identification".

And who is this object? It is the analyst himself, whose mind might not be sufficiently receptive of such projective identifications, or—though receptive—might have been overwhelmed by receiving them, as can often be the case in the primary relationship between infant and mother.

The patient who is prey to fears of annihilation tries to project them into the analyst, in the hope that they can remain in him long enough to be renewed and transformed, but this hope fails if the analyst tries to free himself of them too soon, bringing about an increase in distress and in the projective identifications themselves, which will become ever more violent and undermining of the analyst's mental functioning.

In a sense, what we see here is a description in different words of the model of the mind subsequently postulated by Bion: a mind will be able to develop if there is the capacity to evacuate (project) beta elements (sensorialities) into another mind that will be able to accept them, allow them to stay, and transform them by means of its own containing–transforming capacity into alpha elements (pictograms). These will be restored to the evacuating mind, but together with the method (or the functioning of the method) of alpha function, so they themselves can perform such functions as containment and transformation.

It is a brief enough passage from alpha elements to their concatenation in waking dream-thought, and on into the ability to dream (by day and night). In other words, the sensorialities dealt with by the analyst's capacity for reverie will give life to the development of the mental that coincides with the oneiric, with the ability to dream. Situations of negative reverie which prevent this process can occur if there is a surplus of ♂ contents relative to the ♀ capacity. In these cases—which can be caused by a sort of mental vaginismus in the other, or by an occlusion through excessive anxiety already present in the other's mind (and also simply in a mind too encumbered by theory), or by an excess of projected beta elements—we will have a dysfunction of the whole process which reverie should have brought to the development of the mind (including the capacity for living the emotions), so an inversion of the alpha function will occur, and there will be evacuative phenomena of transformation in hallucinosis.

But let us go back to Bion in 1957 (the year when this paper was presented). He finds himself still straddling two theorisations: one that looks at the object (whether analyst or mother) and its possible dysfunctions, and another that looks at the patient (or infant) as the bearer of a primary "aggression"; which is, however, insufficiently amenable to melioration by the receptive mind of the other (and it cannot be otherwise because the very experience of acceptance can give rise to envy or hatred). The first of these theorisations seems to allow more room for the capacity of a mother–analyst who can accept "nameless dread", or the fear of dying which dwells in the patient and the newborn infant.

Primary destructiveness—or secondary destructiveness following the failure of the earliest relationships? We are very familiar with this unsolved question, which I am tempted to answer in this way: we happen to be a species with a surplus of beta elements and ♂ in relation to alpha function and ♀, as a result of which there persist clusters of beta elements that erupt like uncontainable and untransformable tsunamis which are not destructive in themselves but have inescapably destructive effects on the landscape against which they strike.

Incidentally, we see how a new model or a new theory can come to life, in a sort of titanic struggle between mourning, the capacity to accept transience, and creativity that still causes a degree of catastrophic change in the theories which had briefly reconciled us, as Grotstein (1981) reminds us in his *Do I Dare Disturb the Universe?*

Returning to Bion and his courage in saying that the link between patient and analyst, or between infant and breast, consists in the mechanism of projective identification, I would like to give my paper the title "Attack on the capacities for projective identification". The source of these attacks can be either partner in the analytic or mother–infant couple.

Bion suddenly seems frightened by the inspired direction he has taken, and looks for a compromise that might give him some necessary peace of mind in asserting that innate elements have the greatest importance as far as relationships are concerned; despite the importance of acquired elements, primary aggression and congenital envy remain the pillars.

At this point Bion speaks of "attacks on the analyst's peace of mind", and I see in this emphatic statement, besides the emerging concept of the patient's destruction of the envied good mental functioning of the analyst, the disturbance that the theoretical change of focus and his own genius are causing him in opening up new and (in relation to previous theories) unorthodox thoughts.

97

Well-functioning projective identification enables us to study our own sensations through the effect that they produce in the person who receives them. If this is made impossible, either because the mother is unable to function as a "storehouse" or because hatred and envy prevent the mother from carrying out such a function, then the link between the infant and the breast is destroyed and, as emphasised earlier, the capacity for curiosity is compromised.

If there is an obstruction on the path that would allow the infant to face up to violent emotions, this creates the preconditions for the total elimination of vitality. Every type of emotion brings hatred upon itself until all emotional life vanishes. If the development of emotional literacy fails in the proto-emotional states, the way is opened for de-affective functioning, Asperger's, or autism, with hatred for any form of emotional life, and hatred of life *tout court*.

The centrality of the projective identifications and their vicissitudes becomes ever clearer, not only for mental development, but also for mental functioning and, as I have already pointed out, for the ability to dream, feel, and think.

98

If projective identification fails in its functioning, one of the consequences will be that the external object seems hostile to curiosity and to the "method" with which the newborn tries to satisfy it; this will establish a severe superego, incapable of truth, and an exaltation of moral demands leading to the formation of –(♀♂), which sterilises everything and denies every emotion and all development.

To conclude this part, I would like to say that even if we allow the concept of "an innate destructiveness" (one that is not merely the consequence of a relational failure, however early), I think that at the heart of the matter we would still have the technical problem of how to transform this (supposed) "O" by means of a dream or, rather, by a journey through column 2 of the Grid—that of lying but also of dreams (Grotstein, 2007, 2009)—and of how such an "O" could be transformed by the metabolising digestive activity of that "psychoanalytic field" where it finds itself at work, as a mass of beta elements in search of a dreaming and narrative function.

I would like to play a game in this second part: to see how I might view Bion's clinical material if it were brought to us today. I say "game" both in the sense that it only concerns fragments of material used as examples by Bion himself, and so we, in fact, know hardly anything about them, and in the sense that I enter into it fully aware of being a "dwarf" on the shoulders of a giant, a giant composed of Bion and the theories that he would develop subsequently. This game of mine aims to be an admiring homage and an acknowledgement of how Bion would develop from 1957 onwards. That will be the viewpoint from which I shall play, practising on his "supposed clinical material", at least as I have understood it. (Or, rather, as I have invented it, but I find this useful in showing the generative power of Bion's thought, his theoretical and conceptual monument, which is still waiting to be "absorbed".)

So let me play, bearing in mind that the game can also help us see Bion's model at work.

(A) Bion intervenes to emphasise to the patient the positive feelings he is expressing towards his mother, who had been able to welcome an *insensitive baby* like him.

This interpretation, judging by the patient's response is, to say the least, premature and guilt-inducing (he calls the patient insensitive, and congratulates himself on his own availability to the patient).

The patient, the field's touchstone, responds as if he had received a mouthful too large to swallow, makes movements as if he were having difficulty swallowing, emits gurgling sounds like someone under water, and feels overwhelmed by the interpretation, submerged in it, flooded by it.

I recall that Bion himself (1987), in his *Clinical Seminars*, will say that an interpretation may be given six days, six months, or six years after having been thought, and that an interpretation must match the patient's ability to take it in, otherwise it would be like launching into complex explanations of the functioning of the digestive tract with a baby.

(B) The patient complains that he cannot sleep any more.

Bion suggests that if he slept he might dream.

The patient replies that he feels "wet" and weak.

Bion thinks that feeling wet, soaked, is to do with urine and with the attacks that the patient would have made with his urine through envy and hatred. Looking at the sequence of verbal exchanges, I would have thought of a patient on the alert because he does not know what distressing interpretation might be coming his way, and who, in his fear, is squaring up for a fight.

Here, too, some passages come to mind from the *Clinical Seminars* in which Bion urges us not to give excessively saturated and exhaustive interpretations, and suggests instead that we ask ourselves "Which story is one to tell?" One story that could be told, in my opinion, is that of an infant who is too alarmed to sleep and who, not understanding what his mother is saying to him, drenches himself in pee out of fear.

(C) We do not know how the session starts. Bion considers it reasonable to interpret the patient as being present at a sexual encounter between two people. The patient "reacted as if he had received a violent blow", and Bion gathers that the blow was his interpretation. When the patient seems to have been stabbed with a knife, Bion interprets that he is having hallucinations (of "seeing an invisible object"). Rather than recognising his own interpretation as a knife-blow, Bion disavows his intervention.

We are light-years away from what Bion will say in his *Italian Seminars* (1983): that the patient is capable of describing precisely the analyst's mode of being and operating.

(D) After some isolated remarks ("which had no meaning for me") the patient says he feels understood by a girl he has met, and then shudders.

Bion tries to draw the patient's attention to these shudders.

The patient, in his role as satellite navigation system, replies that the room has been filled with a blue haze: in other words, it seems to me, Bion's attempts had been felt as "polluting".

Here, too, we are in the presence of an analyst who knows too much, who decodes everything instantly. There is not yet the fruit of those "negative capabilities" of which he will speak years later, nor of that extension into the field of myth, passion, and meaning (Bion, 1963) which he talks about in *Elements of Psychoanalysis*.

(E) Bion notes that the patient makes "statements of fact" and adds that Bion would not understand them.

Bion, returning to the contents of the session from the previous day, interprets that the patient feels bad. The patient's response is that he felt there were "two probability clouds" in the room. This would make me think of two possible ways in which the session could develop, or of a weather forecaster confused about the way the weather/session might turn out.

Here, too, we are a long way from the Bion for whom the unsaturated, negative capability, and work towards the "selected fact" will be key points in his way of working.

(F) After half an hour of silence, the patient announces that a piece of metal has fallen on to the floor. I shall pass over Bion's interpretation about envy, saying that perhaps I would have thought the patient means, "It seems to me that a silence like lead or iron has fallen between us."

I merely note that Bion seems in these clinical examples to be looking for a confirmation of the theory he has in mind. Naturally, he is playing a psychoanalytic game (which will later become that inspired psychoanalytic game which is the Grid), putting together a patchwork of different patients and sessions; I have embellished this with my own game, the point of which is to show that Bion's theorising was ahead of its application in the consulting room.

I think, moreover, that all the brilliant later development of his thought and the theorising yet to come are an immense legacy for psychoanalytic theory and technique that we are a long way from having understood and utilised.

In "Attacks on linking", we see a genius at work in the moment of a catastrophic change from theories that are his own and that give him peace of mind, to theories under development that torment him, besides catastrophic changes that allow him new thoughts and new technical formulations.

In saying this, I have in mind *Learning from Experience* (Bion, 1962), *Elements of Psychoanalysis* (Bion, 1963), and *Transformations* (Bion, 1965), but, even more, that wonderful treatise on psychoanalytic technique and theory dramatised as *A Memoir of the Future* (Bion, 1991).

We see in the Bion of 1957 a genius not yet recognised as such, who is making "anticipatory hypotheses" and who dares—while at times retreating into the familiar—to open up the Unknown, the world beyond the Pillars of Hercules, and who will be a Christopher Columbus revealing new and terrible conceptual universes.

I shall now move towards a conclusion, and, in this third part, play another game, which I call "a dwarf on the shoulders of a giant", in which I share some developments of Bion's thought that have occurred to me during an acquaintance of over thirty years with the Bionian oeuvre.

A child in analysis draws for us: Stefano

I shall present some drawings made by a child in analysis, which it seems to me enable us to visualise both the process of his mental growth and to configure a model of the mind that I think is the one we can derive from Bion.

At the first session, Stefano starts by telling a story: there were some skeletons who were walking around in the desert . . . they were an army of skeletons . . . these skeletons had been shot out of caves . . .

I think of Stefano's black rage, how he is turning himself into a robot, his pathological evacuations, his battles with skeletons. But how can I not also think of the mass evacuation of beta elements? How can I not think of primitive projective identifications in search of reverie functions?

Some months later, the drawing shown in Figure 9.2 appears.

Figure 9.1.

Figure 9.2. Head/face/tree.

There is a house in a tree, and a bathroom for doing poos. In the bottom of the tree there is a tunnel. At the bottom of the tree there are bombs that might explode (like proto-emotional states). Inside the tree there is a bomb that has been defused by a bomb-disposal expert. I think of a humanisation, an animation, of an emerging mental functioning, and of the appearance of hollow spaces apart from the newly-created "bathing" function. What is appearing is a mind capable of reverie and able to accept projective identifications, which thereby find a place and become thinkable.

The months pass and the picture shown in Figure 9.3 is drawn during a session.

Between the two trees there is a house suspended on ropes, and reachable by the ropes. The occupants are making soup. Are they expecting guests? A helicopter is transporting a cargo of fruit. In the meantime, they are having a party. How could we not think of a relationality coming to life? We see the arrival of characters and multiple roles, of sociality, of exchange. An emotional field has come to life;

Figure 9.3.

the projective identifications now alphabetised[1] allow the formation of waking dream-thought, and a narrative is comes into being.

Figure 9.4 is the next drawing Stefano made.

In reworking the previous picture (Figure 9.3), Stefano adds some very deep roots underneath, which contain plentiful provisions. In addition, there is a cavern with a disco beneath it and a "reflecting lamp with mirrors", as in real discothèques. Underneath there are rooms for smokers and non-smokers, and other rooms awaiting designation.

How could we not think of the long journey from mechanisation, from beta elements to the constituting of a mental function (alpha), and then the beginning of an ever-stronger relationality that puts down roots with affective contents, and, thereby, develops tools and constructs spaces for fantasy to work in and for generating the unconscious?

Figure 9.4.

Of course, I do not know how this might look from other standpoints, but from my point of view, as an analyst who has observed, and observes, what goes on in the consulting room, the presence of the mind of the other is indispensible for the birth of the psychic. Naturally, the Big Bang of the birth of the psychic other will be followed by the long journey to subjectivise "O", which will become the tolerable "O" for that specific mind and be digested, depending on the enzymes and co-enzymes of which that mind, or, rather, that field, has been able to make use.

The hieroglyphic mother and the Rosetta stone

Carla is a girl aged seven who, on starting school, was found to have a general delay in acquiring language, and difficulty in reading and in memorising the vowels and some consonants.

She has a younger sister who suffers from moments of intense fear.

Their mother is described as warm and affectionate, alternating with moments of emotional incontinence. From the start, there emerges the idea of a child who has had difficulty reading her mother's state of mind, which is now welcoming and receptive and now frankly convex, rebarbative, rejecting. The mother, too, seems unable to find her way among Carla's states of mind, describing her as a puzzling child.

Carla's affective foundation seems disorienting in its alternation of unpredictable emotional states UUUCCU, which have not allowed her a safe standpoint from which to take in these differences: how is Mamma at this moment? What can I expect from her? And also the symmetrical question: what are my feelings towards Mamma? Do I hate her or can I not do without her? The "foundation stone" and its shape are fundamental for the development of the capacity to distinguish another person's emotions (or mental states) and indeed one's own.

The indecipherable mother is an impossible hieroglyph to read in her alternation between concave and convex, partly concave, partly convex.

The situation Carla is exposed to is like driving home and turning into the garage, but never knowing whether the garage door is open or merely a *trompe-l'oeil* against which the car will crash.

We could represent all this with the hypothetical sequence UUCCU or its underlying effective level ♀♀♂♀♂♂♀♀♂.

This narrative of serious difficulties in reading the mind of the other comes up again in a double story begun with great distress by the mother: at school, the teacher told her, Carla seems not to distinguish or recognise even those classmates with whom she has a reasonably good relationship. She goes up to them calling them "Friend" indiscriminately.

There is no clear recognition of Filippo, Luigi, Marcello, just as there is none of the vowels or other letters that she cannot distinguish, and she does not remember whether her tummy sticks out at the front like a "b" or at the back like a "d".

Her father confirms this "reading", recalling their honeymoon in Australia and meeting a variety of people in the house of friends, where nobody was ever formally introduced. Everyone called each other "Mate", creating a certain lack of differentiation.

I should also add the fear felt by a part of her (her younger sister), finding all situations indecipherable.

In the consulting room, is she with a "friend" or a Bluebeard?

What does her grandfather mean when he says "I'll give you a party?"[2]

It is also true that her parents, while lacking in discriminatory function and the ability to identify states of mind, have been sufficiently able to transform the swarms of sensoriality so that Carla had no need for the compulsive focus on details which occurs in the paranoid scenario.

The situation I have described is enacted immediately in the session, where Carla does not know whether she wants to hug or strangle the therapist, and he himself is unable to decipher what the girl is about to do. It is true that the session will become progressively the place of discrimination where Carla and her therapist will learn to understand, accept, and differentiate the components of the fundamental emotional grammar that is being developed as the affective text of the session.

Suddenly Carla goes through a brief period of near-madness in which she fears that people (and emotions) are wearing masks, and that characters are appearing out of a television serial about armed robbers called "the wolf", "the pig", and so on, but Carla tries to evade these by masking her toys.

At the same time, she starts games in which she puts fierce animals (which she is now able to distinguish from tame ones) inside toy saucepans, as if she felt the need to cook them, or, as Bion would say, she lives the need to tame wild thoughts.

The field evolves

The analytic field is also the site of all the patient's and analyst's potential identities, which does not mean that all the potential identities must come to life or be integrated: sometimes it is appropriate for them to remain split off or buried within the strata of the field itself for the whole of the time in which this will be useful for the development of mental life.

For a narrative to develop, as Diderot remembered *à propos Jacques the Fatalist* (1962), there are so many possible stories that must be "put to sleep" so that the main story, the "daughter" of the two co-narrators can come to life and develop.

I have spoken elsewhere of how there are two "loci" of mental creativity in a Bionian metapsychology: the place where beta elements, carriers of all the sensoriality, are transformed via alpha function into pictograms (the sub-units of dream-thought in the waking state) and the place where the derived narrative in all its infinite variety, on a longer or shorter leash, moves away from, or stays close to, waking dream-thought within the field (Ferro, 2002, 2009).

In Simenon's fine novel, *Les Clients d'Avrenos* (1935), the protagonist, Nouchi, tells how when she was a child on her way home from school, she would often observe from behind a fence her sister, only a few years older, giving herself to adult men in exchange for a few coins or chocolate. It was the poor Vienna of the early twentieth century. Then Nouchi becomes an *entraîneuse*, a hostess in a low-life bar, though she remains "frigid".

I have purposely chosen the telling of a neutral episode so as to see the various models at work.

In a model based on historic reconstruction, it is not hard to anticipate where it would take us: to the childhood traumatic experience, child sexuality, abuse, and then the acquaintance with pain.

A model centred on Nouchi's internal world could take us towards eroticised destructiveness and an attack on linking.

An intermediate field model could lead us to a reading like this: an infantile part remains as an observer of what happens in the field; that is, the analyst is coupling with a more adult part of the patient, who gains warmth and sweetness from this but remains nevertheless "cold" because the interpretative coupling has been premature. But I would like to take Ferro further (1999–2014) in order to open up a field understood in a totally different way. That is to say, we do not know it at all: we must merely postulate a field in development, but, in doing so, surrender all its predictability, or at least accept that what we are given to know is F0 (Field 0) while we wait for F1 . . . 2 . . . n.

We cannot, therefore, postulate that the field will be decipherable except in the moment t(0) at which it occurs, but this moment also gives birth to infinite other possible fields that will come to life and be selected by the movement of the potential multitude that is the "couple", and will be knowable only *après-coup* with the opening/closing of infinite possible fields, derivatives of infinite factors, many of which are unknown.

For a long time, too long a time, we thought interpretation was the engine of analysis, an oscillation between time and abstinence/presence and intervention.

The initial episode of which I spoke could, in fact, produce any number of possible stories.

This could be the starting point of an exercise using a range of writings with different outcomes.

Or, equally, different directors could develop different films based on the same outline, the same plot.

(Even if it is not clear what the role of "director" might be in the session or from what it might be constituted.)

From among all the hypotheticals, I would prioritise the "atmospheric" factors of the session and the links formed by multiple and variable reveries with multiple and variable projective identifications.

There is more creativity in not hindering developments than there is in specifically initiating them.

In Sicilian dialect, the term *chiacco* indicates a kind of noose made of rope suspended from wires, usually between opposite or adjacent balconies, for hanging out washing to dry. If something light, a sock or handkerchief, is hung from this it shows the strength of the wind. A patient in analysis tells me that his grandfather used to watch something hanging out to dry so he could see how windy the day was, though the wind was usually a gentle breeze and not the Bora, the north-eastern gale which sometimes batters Palermo.

From the "forecast" given by the movement of something hanging from the *chiacco*, the grandfather would determine the day's risk of catching a cold or cough from the "change of air"—that is, the wind if he was outside, or the dreaded draught if he was indoors.

This could be seen as an anecdote about childhood and as the source of eventual hypochondriac anxieties. Or it could be seen as a warning present in the internal world; or, if seen in moment "0" of the field, as the description of an alarm signal for some emotional current possibly about to come to life.

The description of a field in which possible differences in potential, in temperature, in heat could be dangerous because they would activate currents difficult to control.

In that case the emotions would be winds that could cause illness.

But if we move from time 0 towards time 1. . . and on to "n", we have no way of foreseeing what type of field will develop or what narratives will give meaning to the emotional lines of force that will have come to life. One exercise could be, having set this field to time 0, to describe its possible developments.

In fencing, and even in the very different kind dependent on marking thrusts with electrified jackets and weapons, there is still a basic set of terms: parries, circular parries, hits, feints, double feints, arrests, a "counter", "two counters", and so on, but it is the sum total of these that makes every fencing match—for the knowledgeable spectator—a unique, unrepeatable, and, above all, completely unpredictable experience, because it is the fruit of a combination of variables tending to infinity.

All this could also apply to the development of psychoanalysis, where every change could be experienced as a turbulence to be avoided, even though we cannot evolve without disturbing what we know.

Notes

1. Translator's note: English has no equivalent for *alfabetizzare*, "to make literate", or, in this case, perhaps "to make accessible to literacy". The author is also hinting at the "literal" importance of the alphabet in the case of the next patient, Carla.

2. Translator's note. Carla knows that her grandfather's innocent phrase is also gangster slang: "I'll wipe you out", "I'll waste you".

References

Bion, W. R. (1957). Attacks on linking. *International Journal of Psychoanalysis, 40*(5–6), 308–315.

Bion, W. R. (1962). *Learning from Experience*. London: Karnac.

Bion, W. R. (1963). *Elements of Psychoanalysis*. London: Heinemann.

Bion, W. R. (1965). *Transformations*. London: Karnac, 1984.

Bion, W. R. (1983). *Bion in Rome (Italian Seminars)*. The Estate of W. R. Bion.

Bion, W. R. (1987). *Clinical Seminars and Four Papers*. Abingdon: Fleetwood Press.

Bion, W. R. (1991). *A Memoir of the Future*. London: Karnac.

Diderot, D. (1962). *Jacques the Fatalist*. New York: Collier.

Ferro, A. (1999). *The Bi-Personal Field: Experiences in Child Analysis*. London: Routledge.

Ferro, A. (2002). Some implications of Bion's thought: the waking dream and narrative derivatives. *International Journal of Psychoanalysis, 83*: 597–607.

Ferro, A. (2004). *Seeds of Illness, Seeds of Recovery*. London: New Library/ Routledge.

Ferro, A. (2009). Transformations in dreaming and characters in the psychoanalytic field. *International Journal of Psychoanalysis, 90*: 209–230.

Ferro, A. (2014). *Le Visere della mente. Sillabario emotivo e narrazioni*. Cortina Raffaello.

Ferro, A. (2015). *Torments of the Soul: Psychoanalytic Transformations in Dreaming and Narration*. London: New Library of Psychoanalysis/ Routledge.

Grotstein, J. S. (Ed). (1981). *Do I Dare Disturb the Universe? A Memorial to Wilfred R. Bion*. Los Angeles: Caesura Press.

Grotstein, J. S. (2007). *A Beam of Intense Darkness. Wilfred Bion's Legacy to Psychoanalysis*. London: Karnac,.

Grotstein, J. S. (2009). *But at the Same Time and on Another Level*. London: Karnac.

Simenon, G. (1935). *Les Clients d'Avrenos*. Paris: Gallimard.

Winnicott, D. W. (1974). Fear of breakdown. *International Review of Psycho-Analysis*, 1: 103–107.

INDEX